Henry Luke White of "Belltrees" whose documented
material has provided the basis for this book.

The White Family of

Belltrees

by Judy White

150 YEARS IN
THE HUNTER VALLEY

THE SEVEN PRESS

Welcome to "Belltrees". *Wesley Stacey.*

Designed by Robin James

First published in 1981 by
The Seven Press, Sydney

Typeset in 12/14 Bembo by S.A. Typecentre Pty. Ltd.
Printed by Kyodo-Shing Loong Printing Industries

National Library of Australia
Cataloguing in Publication data
White, Judy.
The White Family of Belltrees.
Includes index.
ISBN 0 9593966 0 8.
1. White family. 2. New South Wales — Genealogy.
I. Title.
929'.2'0994

Contents

Acknowledgements *7*

Introduction *9*

Preface *12*

1. The Beginning of "Belltrees" in N.S.W. *15*
2. W. C. Wentworth and "Belltrees" *23*
3. The Pioneer, James White *27*
4. The White Brothers of "Edinglassie" take over "Belltrees" *37*
5. Consolidation *41*
6. The Partnership *51*
7. The H. L. White Collections *73*
8. Life in the New "Belltrees" Homestead *95*
9. The Culmination of an Era *111*
10. A. H. White *125*
11. Other Families on "Belltrees" *143*
12. Michael Francis White and "Belltrees" Today *159*

The Conclusion *177*

Appendix *180*

Note on Sources *191*

General References *192*

Index *196*

Line-up. *David Moore. Time-Life Books.*

Acknowledgements

I WANT TO THANK the members of the White family of "Belltrees" for the trust they have shown in giving me total access to past records, private documents, letter books, diaries, scrap books, photo albums, wills and strong rooms. Without all these, the "window" onto the past one hundred and fifty years at "Belltrees" would offer little light indeed. To my friend, Verra Woodgate for her invaluable assistance in the reading, cataloguing and cross-cataloguing of fifty-four thousand letters written by H. L. White in fifty-four volumes of Letter Books from 1886-1927, I can only say that without her enthusiasm, constant encouragement and advice this book would never have eventuated.

My sincere gratitude is due to Mr. & Mrs. A. J. Gray for their help and historical knowledge and their permission for me to use the "Gray Collection" of Australian books and manuscripts. I would also like to thank especially Mr. Allan McEvey, Curator of Birds of the National Museum of Victoria, who has written a paper for me on the H. L. White bird-skin and bird egg Collections which appears in Appendix III; and Mr. Tom Darragh, Mr. Frank Coffa, Sandra Evans, Cathy Jordon and Dr. Norman Wettenhall of the same Museum for their help.

Special gratitude is owing to Mr. Tim McCormick, Antiquarian Bookseller of Sydney, for his research into the H. L. White library; to the staff of the Mitchell Library, Sydney and in particular Mr. Paul Brunton of the manuscript department for his transcription of early letters and his account of the H. L. White stamp Collection; to staff of the National Library of Australia in Canberra; and to Mr. David Ferguson of the Mitchell Library, Glasgow, Scotland, Mr. D. B. Colquhoun of Glasgow, Scotland and Mrs. Mary Mackie of "High Belltrees", Renfrewshire, Scotland for historical material pertaining to H. C. Sempill and "Belltrees" in Scotland.

I thank also Mr. Ian Pender, Architect of Maitland, for allowing me to photograph his grandfather's plans of the "Belltrees" homestead which are now in the files of Ian W. Pender & Associates.

I am grateful for the information and enjoyment provided by interviews with Mr. Alec Wiseman, Mr. & Mrs. Cecil McInnes, Mr. Bill Smith, Mr. Bob Sutherland, Mr. Hunter Cobb, Mr. Bruce Minell and all members of our family.

For the loan of paintings, documents and photographs my thanks are extended to Messrs. Richard & Graham White of Guyra, Mr. Reg White of Timor, Mr. Douglass Baglin, Mr. Lance Rossington, Mr. & Mrs. Desmond Vyner, Mr. T. S. W. Jackson, Mr. & Mrs. Alex Cullen, Mr. Jack Ramsay, Mrs. Naida Edwards and Mr. Stuart Hume of "Garroorigan", Goulburn.

To Mr. R. M. Hawkins of Queensland for allowing me to print the reminiscences of his grandfather, Robert Donaldson and to Mr. Noel Layton of the Society of Australian Genealogists for his compilation of the family tree, I offer special thanks. I want to thank Mr. Laurence Le Guay for his encouragement and advice; and especially I thank my typists, Sarah Adams of Sydney, Carol Cassidy of Scone and in particular Judy Ludvik of Sydney. To my niece, Caroline Ryrie, I am grateful for her photographing of members of the family. I am more than appreciative of the patience and co-operation of Robin James who managed to capture the mood of the book I wanted.

I am indebted to my mother, Mrs. Evelyn Crossing, for her encouragement; to Brenda Ogilvie and Kath Merrick who have performed the many and varied household duties that I have neglected over the past two years; and I am delighted that Sir Hermann Black graciously consented to write the introduction.

Above all, I am for ever grateful to Mr. Alan Jones, a family friend and graduate of Queensland and Oxford Universities, who has patiently and diligently edited my text, proof read the final copy and provided a rare interest which has enabled this book to evolve and reach completion.

Introduction

AN INTRODUCTION may be many things . . . an hors d'oeuvre to gastronomic pleasures to follow; or like an overture to opera, as in *Traviata*, float an aural fragment of the elegant and tragic romance to come: or it may be writ to the advice of the Grand Cham of English literature, Dr. Samuel Johnson, who in his usual apodictic manner is recorded in his *Life* by Boswell as saying: "There are two things which I am confident I can do very well: one is an introduction to any literary work, stating what it is to contain, and how it should be executed in the most perfect manner; the other is a conclusion, shewing from various causes why the execution has not been equal to what the author promised to himself and to the public."

I must part company with the good Doctor. I cannot and would not presume to reveal in brief encapsulation what is contained in Judy White's *The White Family of Belltrees. 150 Years in the Hunter Valley*. It is an oeuvre of affectionate, objective history if ever there was one. Nor do I pretend to know the better manner in which the history of a family at "Belltrees" should have been written. So, *pace* to Dr. Johnson.

Judy White has done what she undertook to do, and done it coolly, directly, percipiently, and straight; and all these qualities are strung on a rosary of feeling for this famous Hunter Valley property.

I am not surprised that it is written so. It reveals all the qualities that were latent in the Judy Crossing when she was my student, ere marriage to Michael White, and then seeking her degree in Economics in The University of Sydney.

There is a curious and mysterious process whereby an exercise involving inquiry, set as a task for a student, may play prologue to the future. I recall her responses, revealing qualities then which now come into full flower in this book on "Belltrees".

For myself, I had sat at the feet of the great economist, Joseph Alois Schumpeter, in the Harvard of 1936-37. Deeply influenced by his comprehensive and catholic vision of change and its causes, and in particular the centrality of the role of innovation in shaping development, I remembered with particular force his plea to students to encourage the writing of what he called "monographs", the historical study of a micro-piece of the history and development of some firm, family, farm, enterprise or what have you in an economy. With these intensive particulars as "facts", the grander movements of the whole economy, or a region of it, could be seen in broad outline, but enriched and coloured by particular and personal detail, drawn from these basic units of study.

I sense this work on "Belltrees" is the harvest of her student days, the developed and historical consequence of a taste for serious inquiry acquired in those formative years in working on a setpiece of an exercise.

This book also reveals how one such woman with a different background from that of the spacious Hunter Valley has come to find in the history of "Belltrees" a body of new evidence of how human beings, particularly one notable, continuous family cared and managed it.

Famous names in Australian history have their short and curious involvement with "Belltrees". But one family is linked to this justly famous property; in Judy White's study of a century and a half.

It is fit, proper and welcome that to the studies of the development of Australia should be added this kind of extensive monographic study (in Schumpeter's sense, generously interpreted) by one whose marriage not only drew her into playing her own practical role in the day-to-day operation of "Belltrees", but also led her to research the story of its origins and development to the present.

Those who read these pages, will join her in the retreat, as she calls it, at the top of Mount Woolooma, and will, as it were, hear her tell the story of the White family of Belltrees, and of the future oncoming:

"For their work continueth,
And their work continueth,
Broad and deep continueth,
Greater than their knowing"

SIR HERMANN BLACK, M.EC., HON.D.LITT., F.C.I.S.
CHANCELLOR, The UNIVERSITY OF SYDNEY

WHAT IS SUCCESS? Is it the world's applause?
Sometimes the world applauds with little cause.
Is it, then, titles gain'd or money made?
No! it means something more, indeed, than trade.
Success is always something others grudge,
And so it follows you must be your judge.
You've won success if, when you've run your race,
You leave the world a slightly better place;
If, looking back through years of toil and strife
You feel you've really made the most of life.

Ernest Watt, 1919

Preface

EIGHT YEARS AGO MY HUSBAND, Michael, and I bought the western flank of Mt. Woolooma. This mountain had always been adjacent to "Belltrees" but never part of it. We purchased the land for conservation reasons, to prevent any timber being taken off the escarpment and to protect a colony of Lyrebirds that we knew inhabited the scrubland at the foot of the range. Later we discovered a volcanic outcrop of basalt rocks close by, and one year elapsed before we built a glass and basalt cabin on a prominent ledge, 4,500 feet above sea level. The building was a challenge, but eventually our mountain retreat was completed and we could gaze out over our portion of the Hunter Valley. "Some day," I said to Michael, "I would like to lend this cabin to someone who wants to write a book."

This statement was made seven years ago and yesterday I climbed the mountain in a four-wheel drive Toyota laden with provisions, pencils, paper, tape recorders and data material. Now I sit staring through huge plate glass windows out onto vast tracts of land. To my east are the Barrington Tops and in front of me is the Liverpool Range, with the Glenbawn Dam at centre stage. To my left, partly hidden by immediate hilltops, are the townships of Scone, Aberdeen, Muswellbrook and Singleton. It is to the right of me that I focus particularly, for this is the portion of the topography that I know and understand most. This is "Belltrees" where the Hunter River ambles for many miles through alluvial flats before reaching the Glenbawn Dam. Along the way is the Station block, with vestiges of the present and the past — the stables, the shearing shed, the stockyards, the carpentry shop, the office, the store, the old homestead, the new homestead and the Chapel.

It was here that H. C. Sempill carved out his grant in 1831 and this still remains the nucleus of "Belltrees", the administration centre, 150 years later. As I continue to gaze outwards, my view is interrupted. The sun has risen behind me and casts the huge shadow of Mt. Woolooma over the Valley. It reminds me that the mountain has existed for millions of years and the history about which I write is relatively recent.

I have been hesitant and reluctant to embark on this project but fascinated by the material I have unearthed. However, I am no longer the independent university undergraduate writing her final thesis, knowing that the world stands still until she hands it in. For I am now a wife, a mother of seven children and the housekeeper of a home where the demands are many and the visitors prevalent.

I never dreamt that the person to occupy our retreat and write a book would be me. Yet I have undertaken this task for I realise that the White men themselves, inherently shy and enveloped by modern day pressures may leave forever locked away so much valuable, documented material.

Moreover, when I write about six generations, and their life on the land, I am not just highlighting instances peculiar to "Belltrees". For there are many pastoral families in New South Wales who are trying to maintain the land of their forefathers; trying to overcome seasonal disasters and economic challenges; trying to resist takeovers and resumptions, while maintaining their historical sites and traditions, often only meaningful to the descendants of the families who nurtured them.

The 1980's have brought with them a resources boom; and in the wake of such development, the resources of rural Australia are often forgotten. Great attention has been concentrated on the tribal rights of Aboriginal people and a new recognition is being shown for the reverence they hold for their birth place. Both these developments are essential. But we must never overlook the tremendous affinity that whitemen have for their soil, their land and the places where they were born. It is imperative that Governments, companies and communities understand the deep feelings of country people.

As I write this, many country properties including "Belltrees" are in the grip of one of the worst droughts on record. Indeed, since records were kept on "Belltrees" over 150 years ago, average annual rainfall has never been lower than it is now. It will take many years for farmers in many areas to recover. But the records also show how the old hands survived the bad seasons of the past, never overstocking their country and laying down ensilage pits to enable future generations to keep their stock alive. These blueprints are invaluable — for comparison, for posterity and for pride. Well-kept station diaries are a "must" for any successful pastoral undertaking.

This book is not a total history, but a window onto history. It is born of my nostalgia for the past and my determination to unlock some of its doors. My efforts have been inspired by the hope that this story may activate, in those alive today, a sense of pride for what past generations have achieved over 150 years on "Belltrees" — not just the White family but all families who have contributed to the history of this property. In this way the book is written as a testimony and a tribute.

H. C. Sempill, Esq by Charles Rodius
(England 1827). *Courtesy Mitchell Library.*

CHAPTER ONE

The Beginning of "Belltrees" in N.S.W.

IN 1830, THE PIONEER HAMILTON COLLINS SEMPILL, came to Australia. The following year, he received a primary grant of 2,560 acres at the junction of the Hunter River and Woolooma Gully. He named it "Belltrees". Through this name, hundreds of years of Scottish history were transplanted into New South Wales. The Sempill name itself is part of Scottish antiquity. The first "Semple" on record flourished in the reign of King Alexander II who succeeded to the Crown of Scotland in 1214. Since the middle ages, the name "Bultreis" appears in Scottish Church records.[1] In 1545 William, the second Lord Sempill, obtained a charter of land in the Belltrees area of Scotland from Queen Mary. From that time on, the Sempill family and Belltrees were synonymous, so much so that Scottish tutors referred to the young Sempills in their charge as "young Belltrees".[2]

The obvious beauty of this environment, and the union between Sempills and Belltrees is clearly illustrated by a recent Scottish chronicler:

> " The sight of Belltrees nestling snugly in a fold in the hills reminds us that the district's association with the Sempills is never far away. Down there, in that pleasant retreat which has changed little over the years, many illustrious scions of the family were born, some of whom were to play great roles in the history of their native land . . . The beauty of the countryside around Belltrees is so great that it is not difficult to realise how much inspiration the Sempills derived from their pleasant surroundings . . . Clear streams flowed noisily through dark glens and rushed headlong across green fields and meadows, above which the exuberant song of the hovering skylark could be heard; and now and again a robin and wren would appear suddenly on a gatepost and scold angrily at the intruder who dared to enter his territory."[3]

H. C. Sempill possessed a vision to create such a scene in Australia, though at the time he chose the name his star was not high with the Scottish Sempills of Belltrees. For H. C. Sempill, although heir to the wealth of his granduncle Robert Sempill, was not a Sempill at all but, in actuality, Hamilton Collins. But Robert Sempill had outlived his own children and a condition of his will was that, in order to inherit Robert Sempill's wealth, Hamilton Collins was to assume his mother's maiden name of Sempill. This he did and within eight years of Robert Sempill's death, Hamilton Collins Sempill had squandered his inheritance. He had no alternative but to look to Australia which beckoned him as a land of promise in which money could be made quickly rather than as a place in which he would live permanently.

Whilst still in England, H. C. Sempill was selected to take over as Manager of Mr. Potter Macqueen's 20,000 acre estate, "Segenhoe", in northern New South Wales. John Beavan, solicitor to Potter Macqueen in England, chose H. C. Sempill and described him as, "a clever, industrious, cunning man who would live and make a fortune on a mountain brow where others would starve."[4]

The well known Scone historian, Nancy Gray, has described H. C. Sempill's voyage to Australia:

> "Sempill chartered a ship, THE WARRIOR and filled it almost to overflowing with paying passengers — 'gentlemen of respectability', their wives and families, their menservants and maidservants, their horses, pigs, sheep and cattle. On the 13th March, 1830, most of the passengers disembarked at Fremantle, complaining bitterly of their treatment at Sempill's hands. They had little chance of redress for while they were making formal complaint THE WARRIOR sailed for Sydney."[5]

H. C. Sempill, his wife, children and servants landed in Sydney on May 29, 1830, and within a month or two were in residence at "Segenhoe" near Scone. It was not long before H. C. Sempill decided to open up and acquire more land for himself. The early 1830's were boom years and emigrants with initiative were able to acquire vast holdings. H. C. Sempill thrived on his new venture. He followed the Hunter River from "Segenhoe" to its head at "Elistoun" later "Ellerston" and during the journey acquired many grants — 1,150 acres at "Ardenhall"; 910 acres at the junction of Redbank Creek; a further 1,200 acres near Taylor's Creek; 1,280 acres at "Huntingdon", opposite Donald's Creek; 715 acres at "Aberfoyle", on the junction of Brushy Hill Creek and 640 acres at the junction of the Page's Creek and the Hunter River, which he named "Elistoun", another historical name from Renfrewshire in Scotland which dates back to the middle ages. A

Above: "Belltrees – Hunter River, New South Wales – residence of H. C. Sempill Esq.," Watercolour c. 1835. Artist unknown. *Courtesy Dixson Gallery.*

Right: Aerial view of "Belltrees" showing station block, shearing shed, homestead, the Hunter River and Mt. Woolooma. *Trevor Lott.*

Above: The White cottage, built by H. C. Sempill 1832. *M. F. White.*

Left: The main bedroom of the original homestead is now an office. *Laurence Le Guay.*

further 560 acre purchase on Bell's Brook, firstly named the village of Macqueen, is now known as Moonan Flat. Amongst all of these was the grant of 2,560 acres known as "Belltrees". Having acquired all these "key" positions and abundant land on the Hunter, Sempill looked for other green pastures in the New England region. It was H. C. Sempill who first occupied the area he named Walcha.

Although often described as a rogue and an overbearing character, tactless in his attitude towards his fellow settlers, H. C. Sempill's land acquisitions were indeed impressive during his brief twelve year stay in the colony. By 1840, the generally bad times had claimed many victims. H. C. Sempill was amongst them. Banks demanded immediate repayment on money they had previously been anxious to lend, while drought conditions caused a general decline in the pastoral industry. For the flamboyant adventurers, who were fired by the promise of early gains, prospects were grim. H. C. Sempill returned to Scotland, ostensibly to procure the emigration of shepherds from the Highlands; but he remained there, a victim of the hungry Forties. In March 1844, he advertised the sale of his stations at Walcha and Dungowan Creek; and stock at "Elistoun", "Belltrees", "Aberfoyle", "Long Flat" and "Hornsdale". It was a time when land was changing hands at depressed prices for large acreages. It was a time for the resourceful and opportunistic W. C. Wentworth to build upon his already impressive empire.

Given more favourable conditions, H. C. Sempill may have been remembered more as a nation builder than as a member of the British gentry who returned home and died in poverty. Certainly, whilst he owned "Belltrees", he constructed some interesting old buildings which remain intact 150 years later. In 1832, he built a small cottage with sandstock bricks, "The White Cottage", the first building on "Belltrees". It was probably built with the assistance of masons, sawyers and carpenters, assigned convicts from "Segenhoe". Its design is simple and enchanting. On the wooden doorways, which are about 5′ 8″ high, are convict engravings, lasting evidence of the early builders. The cottage was used by surveyor Robert Dixon when he traced the course of the Mt. Royal Range in 1832[6] and it remains in use today.

H. C. Sempill had improved the living quarters at "Segenhoe" soon after he arrived in 1830. In August, 1834, Mr. Potter Macqueen arrived in New South Wales, following the death of his wife in France. Within three months, "Segenhoe" was host to Governor Major-General Richard Bourke and the pageantry surrounding his welcome, so obviously the work of H. C.

Sempill, is colourfully recorded in the Sydney Herald of November 24, 1834:

> ". . . Mr. Macqueen with his carriage and four . . . brought His Excellency to 'Segenhoe'. On reaching a certain point where the first glimpse of 'Segenhoe' is obtained, the carriage was met by 26 horsemen . . . the speed of the avant courier was checked by the immediate discharge of canon, and the hoisting of the British flag in different positions . . . the carriage moved on . . . at a very slow pace through a line on one hand, of 144 working bullocks yoked up to 18 iron ploughs with drivers and ploughmen in new suits of clothing; (and) on the other hand (of) 18 drays with shaft bullocks and their attendants. Further on, stood eight teams yoked up to harrows, scufflers, and other implements of husbandry; and opposite to these, eight pack bullocks with their packs, loaded for the distant outstations; further in advance, stood the native chief of 'Segenhoe' with 40 followers, painted in the most grotesque manner, carrying spears of twelve to fourteen feet long, and other implements of war; and eight black boys each holding a couple of kangaroo dogs. Opposite to David, King of 'Segenhoe', stood 'Duwaroo', Chief of 'Waverley', flanked by 40 Blacks of his own tribe, having also their instruments of war, and eight black boys each holding a leash of kangaroo dogs. His Excellency passed on through the inner gates midst the roaring of the canon and the deafening cheers of the establishment where Mr. Sempill was in waiting to receive him . . ."[7]

H. C. Sempill's family had occupied the main homestead at "Segenhoe" but soon were unceremoniously removed to make way for Mr. Macqueen and his female companion, Madame Ramus. The Sempill's new accommodation was crude and Mrs. Sempill became ill. H. C. Sempill then decided to build more permanent buildings including a homestead at "Belltrees". Part of that homestead still stands at the bottom of the garden today. Regrettably, one wing, although in perfect condition, was pulled down in 1908 to make way for a croquet lawn. The kitchen is today a museum; the laundry, a carpentry shop; and the main bedroom, an office. Mrs. Sempill, still unwell, preferred to live in her Sydney home "Rockwall" amid eight acres at Woolloomooloo while H. C. Sempill made only periodic visits to his Hunter River properties.

His superintendent, John Mitchell, occupied "The White Cottage". John Mitchell had come to Australia with Sempill on THE WARRIOR as his manservant; and later, John Mitchell's son was the first child to be born at "Belltrees". Descendants of his live today in a cottage adjacent to "The White Cottage". In 1840, John McIver and his wife moved into the homestead. In that year, the McIvers were witnesses to the first marriage at "Belltrees" and on the same day, their daughter, Marie, became the first child to be

The White cottage built 1832. *Wesley Stacey*.

White wisteria now grows outside the office.
This was part of the original homestead. *John Smith.*

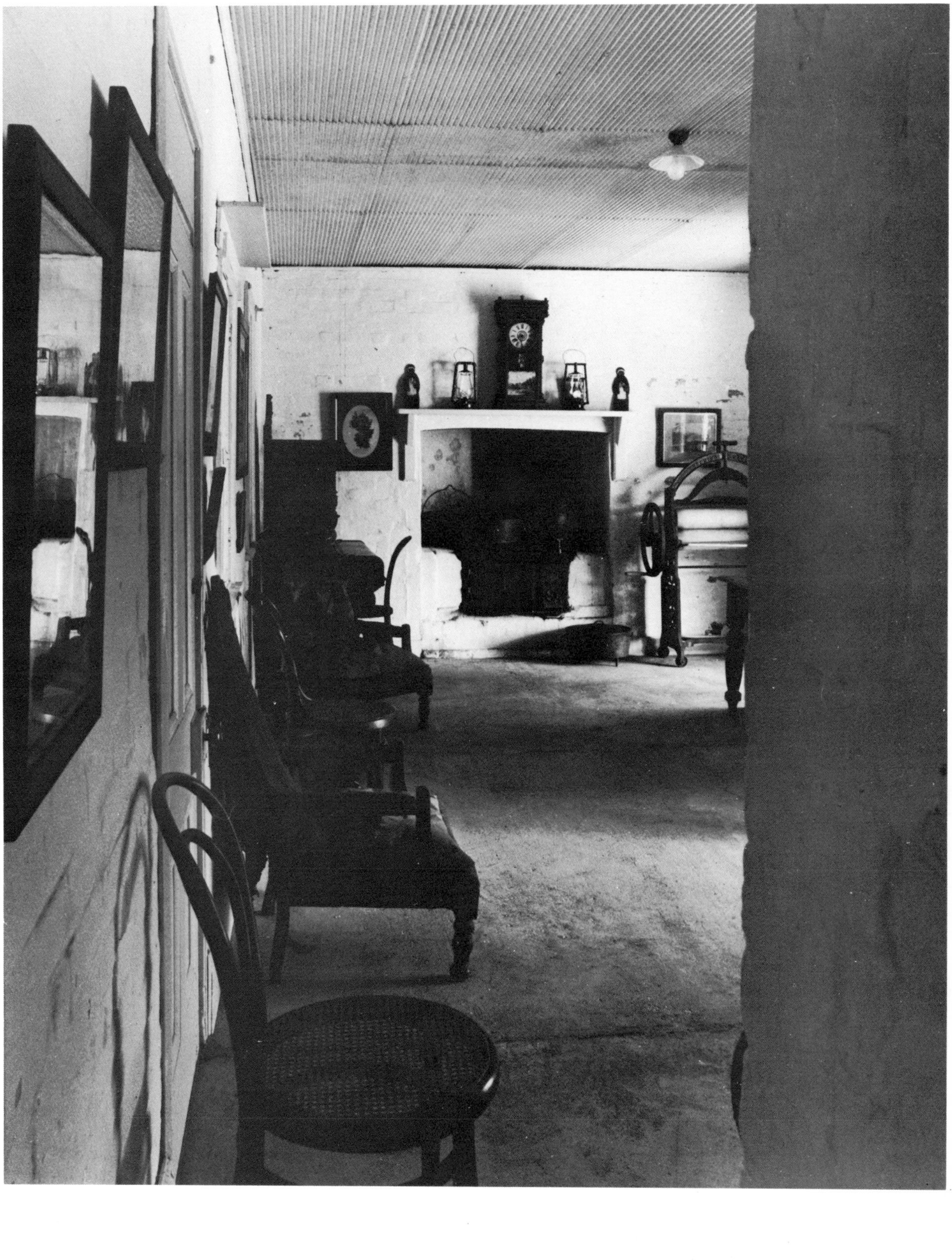

The old kitchen is now a museum. *Wesley Stacey.*

baptised at "Belltrees".[8] Under the guidance of H. C. Sempill, "Belltrees" was becoming more than a sheep run. It was taking shape as a community. The 1841 census records that even then there were 26 people on "Belltrees" including convicts and shepherds.

It is difficult to imagine the Valley in the early decades of the last century — heavily timbered and totally unfenced. Each night the shepherds had to herd their sheep together to protect them from dingoes or Aborigines descending from the higher hills. Flocks had to be carefully nurtured as there were no known chemical cures for foot rot, scab or catarrh which often took charge of and decimated sheep herds. The Hunter Valley was nothing more than waste land which had remained in its primitive state for millions of years. The country was uncharted and unknown. There were no roads, no cars, no communications. Men on horseback faced, like shepherds, the prospect of being ambushed by bushrangers, escaped convicts, Aborigines or wild dogs. Rural labourers were hard to find, the more intelligent convicts or emigrants preferring to remain near their port of disembarkation. On top of this, by 1840, the transportation of convicts was stopped, creating even greater scarcities of labour in rural areas.

H. C. Sempill confronted all these obstacles and was able to transform "Belltrees" from virgin country into a substantial sheep run. However, by the 1840s, with emigration checked and unlimited credit discontinued, general panic ensued. Almost the whole colony fell into public bankruptcy and H. C. Sempill proved unable to escape this fate. He returned to Scotland leaving his son Robert to manage his affairs. But by 1844 Robert was forced to relinquish "Belltrees" and this by now impressive estate passed from the losing hand of an aspiring pioneer into the full pack of a prosperous politician. The H. C. Semphill era had ended and the realm of W. C. Wentworth was extended.

The Liverpool, London & Globe Insurance plaque, 1836 on the iron-bark slab store.
Laurence Le Guay.

CHAPTER TWO

W. C. Wentworth and "Belltrees"

W. C. Wentworth, Esq.
Courtesy Mitchell Library.

HISTORIANS DIFFER on the manner by which W. C. Wentworth came into possession of "Belltrees". One thing is certain — whatever dealings Wentworth had with H. C. Sempill or his son, Robert Sempill, they were not amicable. An original letter of November, 1845 from W. C. Wentworth to Robert Sempill, only recently unearthed in the "Belltrees" library, demonstrates the rancour with which correspondence between the two men was exchanged. "I find you acting very improperly with respect to Belltrees and the adjoining runs," it says. Wentworth's letter makes mention of a law suit pending between him and Sempill over the ownership of "Belltrees" and argues that, "I cannot allow you to be wantonly burning down huts transferred to me . . . If you persist in such conduct as this," Wentworth continues, "I shall be obliged to rent all the government ground around you and eat you out . . ."[1]

Robert Sempill was not going to leave "Belltrees" without protest and chose, at least for the time being, to ignore the rights of Wentworth as mortgagee of the property, a status derived from his taking over H. C. Sempill's debts upon the latter's departure for Scotland. Wentworth's letter to H. C. Sempill's son continues:

> "Your unauthorised occupation of any part of the house or other premises at Belltrees can have no effect whatever on the ultimate fate of the law suit. Mr. McIver admitted you into the house as a guest and I have no objection, if it is a matter of convenience to you, to allow you to remain for the present in the occupation of the room you have there but . . . as I stand in the position of the mortgagee of this estate and as such have an undoubted right to the possession, I shall on my going to Belltrees assert that right, in a proper manner. If you or your servants attempt to interfere

with it, I only regret that I shall be driven to adopt extreme measures to bring you to reason."[2]

This stinging letter to Robert Sempill obviously had little effect for on March 5, 1846 Wentworth wrote from Vaucluse to the Government Surveyor seeking the means to prevent Sempill from moving his stock from "Ellerston" to "Belltrees". By buying up land in between, such movement could only be achieved by Sempill's trespassing on Wentworth's property. Wentworth's letter to the Surveyor also makes more explicit his contempt for the British aristocracy or the "gentry" as he called them.

> ". . . I wish to have two or three, 40 or 50 acre allotments measured at Butcher's Flat and Moonan Creek so as to render it impossible for young Sempill to drive his sheep out or in from the station . . . without trespassing on some portion of my land. Though this will doubtless be an expensive way of getting rid of these gentry, I find I have no other alternative left to me . . ."[3]

W. C. Wentworth had his problems in trying to complete the transaction of the "Belltrees" settlement. He encountered numerous setbacks from the previous owners, who obviously did not wish to relinquish their land and possessions. Added to this, Wentworth himself had a dislike for the British gentry in general, and for the Sempill attitude in particular. He had already suffered at the hands of the "exclusives" in the colony of New South Wales, and was embittered towards their class status. His dislike of them lay deep within him, and affected his political thoughts and actions. In particular he fought for the ownership of the Australian colony's wastelands to be made available to Australian "settlers" rather than granted to the British aristocracy. Wentworth later won through in his fight for the rights of Australian squatters and brought about great changes in land legislation in New South Wales. W. C. Wentworth was the son of a convict girl and a medical practitioner. His patriotism made him a controversial figure in his fight for the status of Australian-born within the new colony. In a speech to the New South Wales Legislative Council in 1853, he argued passionately that a,

> ". . . powerful body will be formed of men of wealth, property and education — men not raised from any particular section of the community but from every class that has the energy to aspire to rank and honour . . ."[4]

There is no doubt that Wentworth possessed an insatiable desire for new holdings. By 1854 he had amassed great wealth and was the largest landholder in New South Wales. Since the death of his father D'Arcy Wentworth in 1827, and up until his departure for England in 1854, W. C. Wentworth had added fifteen large sheep stations, including "Belltrees", to his inheritance. But one of his most ambitious plans was thwarted by Governor Sir George Gipps in 1840. Wentworth and some associates had attempted to procure one-third of New Zealand from Maori chieftains. It was a deal which involved 100,000 acres in the North Island and 20 million acres in the South Island. But for the intervention of Gipps, Wentworth would have been the greatest land owner in the world.[5]

During his ownership of "Belltrees", 180,000 sheep were shorn and washed annually at the station — not just "Belltrees" sheep but sheep from his other runs at Cassilis, Kickerbill, Coolah and Gammon Plains. As wool was then washed on the sheep's back, the long distances across which these sheep travelled was justified to Wentworth by the superior washing facilities at "Belltrees". In modern times the extent of Wentworth's holdings defies comprehension. By 1848 his stock runs in New South Wales included almost 140,000 acres on the Liverpool Plains; over 220,000 acres in County Bligh; and 197,000 acres near Wellington.[6]

Wentworth was equal to the challenge created by the 1840's.[6] In 1844 he set up a huge boiling down works at Windermere near Maitland capable of handling 1,000 sheep or 80 cattle at a time. This was a difficult period. When the price of stock fell drastically, Wentworth helped other squatters overcome bankruptcy by boiling down sheep and cattle for tallow which was then selling in London for £26 a ton.[7] But above all Wentworth perceived the need for land reform and entered the Legislative Council of New South Wales in 1843. He was an orator of immense power and prestige and led the squatters in the demand for new land regulations. They wanted security of tenure so that they could improve their runs without fear of displacement. The Imperial Act of 1846 was the first step in this direction. The Act enabled squatters to purchase key sites on their runs such as those around water courses and waterholes. This gave them a control over their holdings that previously they were only able to lease and offered a new sense of permanence to men on the land. The Imperial Act brought to an end the early age of the squatter.

Cementing this change, the British Parliament in 1852 successfully moved that it was the wish of the representative Legislative Council in New South Wales that the Crown make an unconditional surrender of lands to the colony. One of Wentworth's sternest critics on this issue, Dr. John Dunmore

Lang, described this move as "the fatal mistake" arguing that the Legislative Council in New South Wales was not a truly representative body of people but a mere clique of squatters. Dr. Lang saw this as a dramatic shift in power from the Crown to the colony and in particular warned that enormous financial power was now vested in the New South Wales Government.

The fact that Wentworth owned "Belltrees" when he was formulating important land Acts within the Legislative Council of New South Wales, adds an extra dimension to "Belltrees" history. For these Acts had a far reaching effect on this particular estate and on other similar holdings throughout New South Wales. Wentworth's drive and sheer financial strength enabled him, above all others, to hold onto "Belltrees" and ride out the desperate years between 1844 and 1848. Wentworth had not lived on "Belltrees" or even managed it for long, but the Wentworth era was an interesting one. "Belltrees" had been expanded and utilised in conjunction with other runs and pastoral vistas in New South Wales had been expanded.

The stage was now set for the White brothers when they took command of "Belltrees" from Wentworth to move forward in a favourable economic position. Wentworth had placed it within the squatters' rights to purchase the key positions on their runs and command the right to adjoining lands. This naturally gave way to a period of rapid pastoral expansion not only in the Upper Hunter but generally throughout New South Wales. In crude terminology, the era of "dummying" and "peacocking" had begun and the White brothers, James, Francis and George of "Edinglassie", Muswellbrook, were not hesitant in taking advantage of their strategic position by acquiring vital land grants along the Hunter River and its tributaries. "Belltrees" was entering a boom period.

CHAPTER THREE

The Pioneer, James White

IN 1831, THE SAME YEAR THAT H. C. SEMPILL acquired "Belltrees", James White took possession of his primary grant of 1,280 acres at the junction of the Isis and Page Rivers, five miles away. He named it "Broomfield" after his English home in Somerset. James White had left Somerset having been commissioned in early 1826 by the Australian Agricultural Company to take 79 valuable French merino sheep from the homeland to the new colony. Some of the history of the Australian Agricultural Company is worth recalling for the Company had a profound effect on the opening up of vast tracts of virgin country in Australia.

In 1819, the Colonial Secretary, Earl Bathurst, commissioned John Thomas Bigge to prepare a report for the British Government on the state of the colony of New South Wales, and in particular to offer advice as to how the convict situation could best be handled in this new continent. Several years later, Commissioner Bigge returned to England confirmed in the view that it would be more economical for the government to assign convicts to free settlers and recommended that grants of land be given to such settlers in proportion to the number of convicts they were prepared to employ and the number of sheep and cattle they took with them. The purpose of Bigge's recommendation was to induce persons of respectability to engage personally in the rearing of sheep and cattle on an extensive scale in Australia's inland, and to attract capital and expertise to the colony. The substance of Bigge's report, together with the enthusiasm of John Macarthur Jnr. for what he knew to be Australia's capacity for fine wool production, led to

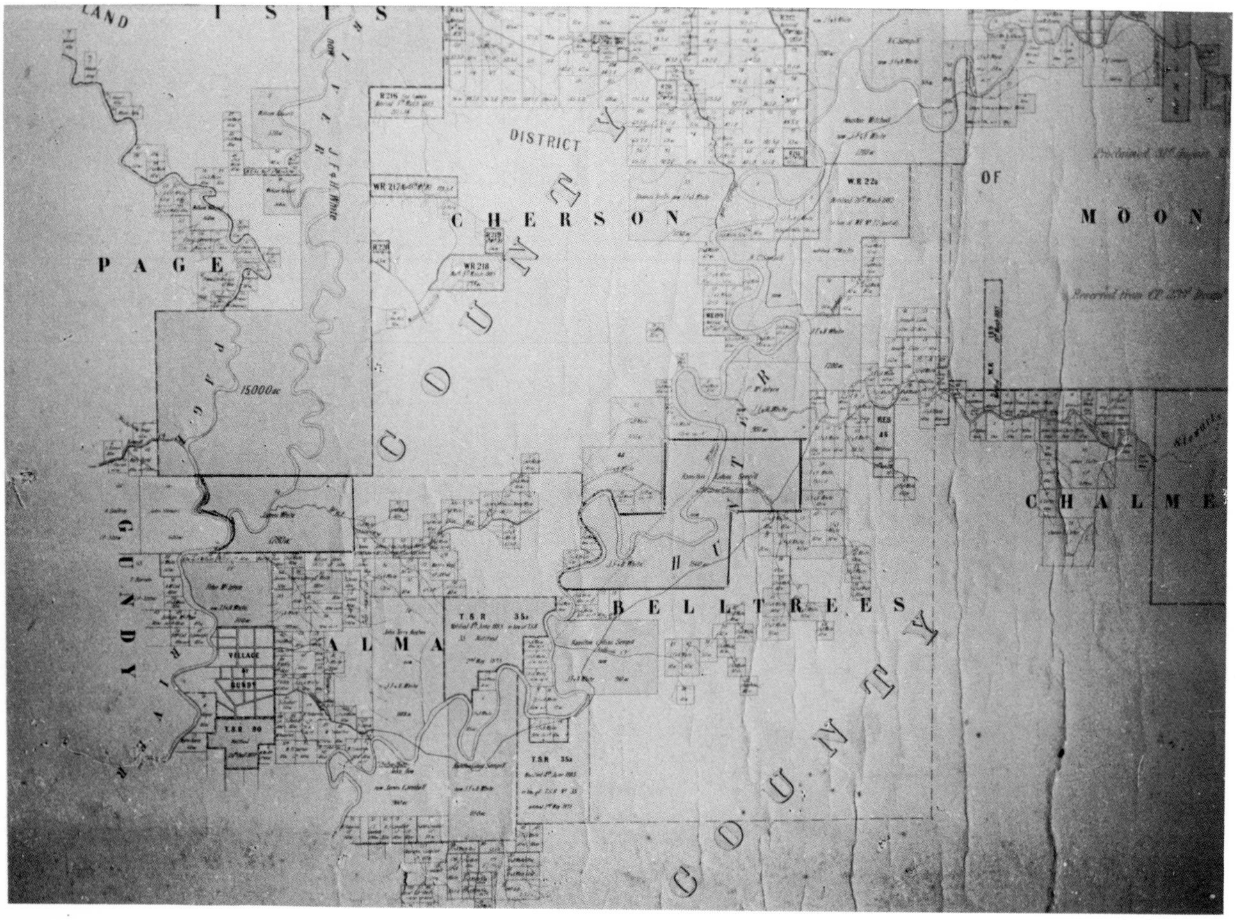

Section of map showing the two primary grants of 1831 – 1,280 acres to James White on the junction of the Isis and Page Rivers; 2,560 acres to H. C. Sempill on the junction of the Hunter River and Woolooma Gully. *H. L. White. 1884.*

the promotion in 1824, in London, of the idea of an Australian Agricultural Company.

The Bigge Report and Macarthur's enthusiasm influenced the British Parliament on June 28, 1824 to pass an Act granting certain powers and authorities to a company to be incorporated by charter and to be called the Australian Agricultural Company, for the purpose of cultivating and improving the wasteland of the colony of New South Wales. The Act further provided that the Australian Agricultural Company be given, by the Crown, one million acres of land, free of charge, anywhere in Australia. By doing this, it was hoped that 1,400 convicts would be employed by the Company thereby diminishing the cost to government expenditure to the extent of over £30,000 annually.

The Australian Agricultural Company remains today the largest landholder in Australia. Following the British Parliament's approval of the formation of this Company, John Macarthur appointed John Dawson as the Company's agent. He arrived in Sydney in December, 1825 with forty men and women, sheep and horses. He moved with a haste which denied the exercise of thorough investigation and established the headquarters of the Company around Port Stephens. It was only a matter of a few months later that James White left England aboard the "Fairfield" with the Company's flock of valuable merinos.

James White was then only 25.[1] He accepted the job of bringing these stud sheep to Australia with a deep sense of responsibility and with a genuine care for the stock in his charge. Throughout the voyage he recorded, each evening, the condition of every sheep. His detailed diary of the voyage, in the Mitchell Library, makes fascinating reading.[2] It demonstrates not only the ravages of such a long voyage on the flock; but also the diary is a testimony to the tenacity and discipline of the man — qualities abundantly demonstrated in successive generations of his descendants.

James White landed the sheep safely at Port Jackson, and then escorted them to the Australian Agricultural Company's settlement at "Retreat Farm", Parramatta, and thence to Port Stephens. For three years, from 1826 to 1829, he worked as Sheep Superintendent for the Company. The early years were exceedingly difficult. The job of training convicts to become shepherds and rural labourers was beyond the capabilities of Mr. Dawson. The one million acre grant at Gloucester, selected for the production of fine wool, proved inadequate and too light with the result that the standard of the stock suffered. James White soon realised that it was impossible to regain and retain the standard of the stock under such adverse conditions. The British manufacturers and London shareholders were becoming anxious. In 1829, Mr. Dawson was recalled to England, and the Company, awaiting the arrival of Sir Edward Parry, passed into the temporary control of James Ebsworth, the Assistant Commissioner.[3]

It is interesting to note at this point that many years later, in the late 1880's, three White brothers, grandchildren of James White, married three Ebsworth sisters, grandchildren of James Ebsworth.

At the same time that James Ebsworth took over temporary control of the Australian Agricultural Company, James White left the Company to become Sheep Manager to one of its Colonial Directors, Dr. James Bowman. Dr. James Bowman had succeeded D'Arcy Wentworth as principal surgeon of the colony in 1819. He married Mary, daughter of John Macarthur, who was the original propounder of the importance of the wool trade to Australia. With a dowry of stock from the Macarthur family, Dr. and Mrs. James Bowman set up the large estate of "Ravensworth", near Singleton in the Hunter Valley. James White and his wife moved there with the Bowmans. While their eldest son, James, was born at Stroud in 1828, five of their sons were born at "Ravensworth" — Francis in 1830; George in 1831; William Edward in 1834; Frederick Robert in 1835, and Henry Charles in 1837; while Edward was born at their permanent home, "Edinglassie" near Muswellbrook in 1839, the year it was purchased by James White.[4]

The hazards of colonial bush life for English brides like Mrs. James White cannot be underestimated. Such women stepped onto strange soil after a rigorous sea voyage. They clung to their former way of life in a land vastly different from their homeland. They wore dresses totally unsuitable to the new climate; they planted English botanical species only to see them wither and die. Daily they awaited news from home when their only link with England came via mail bags aboard ships which arrived at irregular and infrequent intervals. So often these women lived in total fear of unpredictable encounters with ex-convicts, Aborigines, snakes, spiders and insects. Above all, there was the ever-present fear of unaided childbirth. Still-birth and infact mortality were prevalent. One only has to study any early family tree to assess the relationship between the number of children born in the colony at the time to the number who lived.

Silhouette of the pioneer, James White. *Belltrees Library*.

So it was that in 1826 Mrs. James White (née Sarah Crossman) lost her first child, a daughter named Jane. Nonetheless Sarah White gives little indication of being an English hothouse flower.

For the first three years, from 1826 to 1829, James and Sarah White lived at Stroud on the Australian Agricultural Company's one million acre Gloucester estate. It could hardly have been an enjoyable experience. The experiment of assigning convicts to men of respectability lacked any system or proper supervision. For a start, the convicts did not understand the land — land which was forbidding country in which to nurture a sheep flock. Sheep were not counted, stallions ran wild and the Company's stock inevitably deteriorated. Often convicts became rebellious and the Company's agents simply could not cope. James Bowman, a Colonial Director of the Australian Agricultural Company, decided to utilise James White's sheep expertise on his own lands and for almost ten years, from 1829 to 1839, James White managed Dr. Bowman's "Ravensworth" estate and his adjoining runs. This did not preclude James White from acquiring holdings of his own or from increasing his own stock herd.

By this time, James White's brother Edward had arrived from England aboard THE HARRIET and was also employed by James Bowman. James White had arrived in Australia in 1826 with at least £500 and some of his own stock. By 1830 he was in a position to make application to the Colonial Secretary for a grant of his own. This application received strong support from Dr. Bowman in his dual capacity as employer of James White and Colonial Inspector of Hospitals. In supporting correspondence to the Land Board, Bowman spoke of James White as "a very steady, competent and respectable young man . . . in my employment one year and ten months and (receiving) £100 a year . . ."[5] The grant was approved and James and Edward White were authorised to take possession of "Broomfield" on October 18, 1831. They began operation from that date although the actual title deeds were not issued until September 23, 1839. Edward White, in keeping with the undertaking given in his brother's application, agreed to live on the "Broomfield" grant. In 1832, the brothers were assigned convicts to work on "Broomfield". They cleared the country and built post and rail fences and in return received food and clothing as payment.

James and Edward White were fortunate that the Aborigines close by at Gundy Gundy (meaning "Big Camp") were not a war-like tribe. There were sixteen men, eight women and five children in the camp. They were the Murrawin tribe and hunted along the Page's River. Evidence of the Murrawin tribe's presence

After settling in we needed some supplies so we hea came across a French Restaurant and thought that r decided to look at the menu in the window and see the restaurant to see what it looked like inside. Sud restaurant appeared and asked could he help us. W food so he invited us inside so he could explain the later in the week which we were looking forward to

As we got chatting we told him we were on our hon day to hire a car. He said "the train only runs in the and the hire cars were so expensive". He said he kn road and he would hire out a little car he had there tell him you are friends of mine and see what he ca

So we spoke to the Petrol Station owner and we we said he had a Renault that we could use". When we week". We were astounded but very happy to have

We had a lovely time in this car going to different p went for a trip to the Kangaroo Valley a place I had As we climbed the hill before descending in the val of people behind us and they were getting really fr stopped I went to pull the hand brake on and foun we had been going so slowly.

Jane Baker 1769.

(59) Crowcombe
Somerset

Death Bef 21 May 1813.
Crowcombe Somerset.

James 28 Nov 1765
Crowcombe Somerset.

---

55 fives

Sunshine Coast.

Above: The original Belltrees homestead still stands at the bottom of the garden. *M. F. White*.
Right: The old kitchen is now a museum. *Laurence Le Guay*.

The slab store. c. 1835. *Douglass Baglin.*

Sarah White (née Crossman). *Kindly lent by Mr. Reg. White, Timor.*

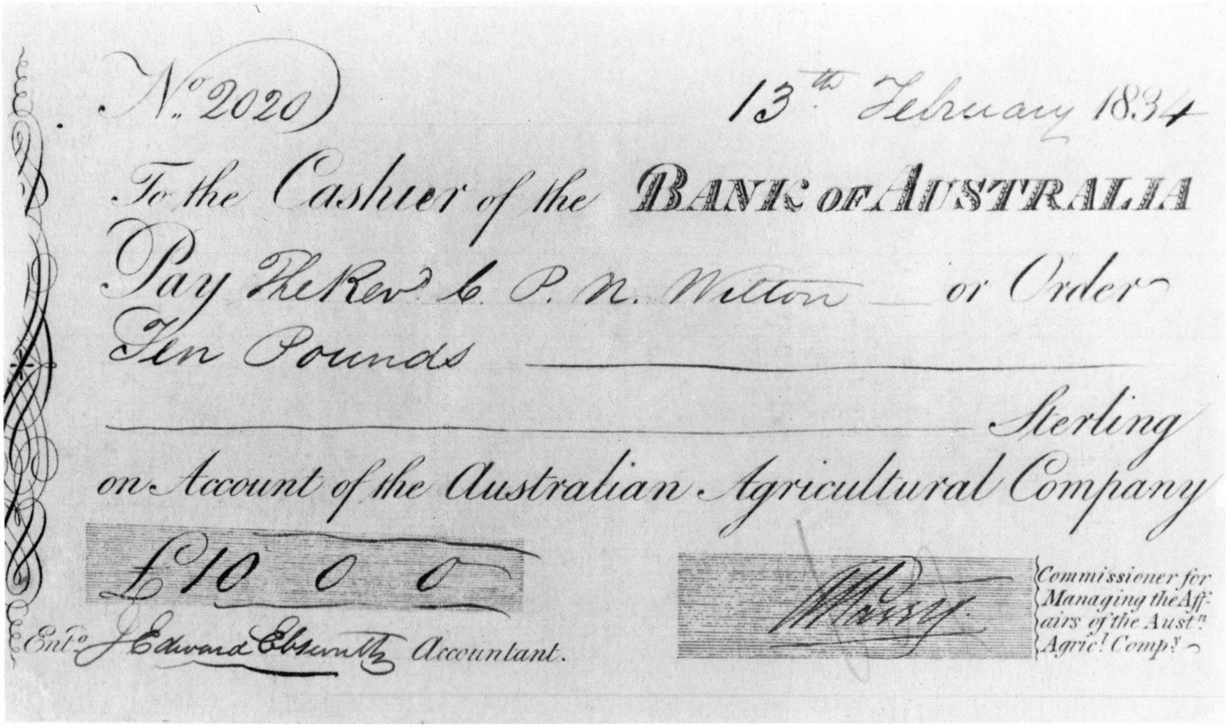
No. 2020 13th February 1834
To the Cashier of the BANK OF AUSTRALIA
Pay The Revd. C. P. N. Wilton or Order
Ten Pounds
Sterling
on Account of the Australian Agricultural Company
£10 0 0
W. Parry
Commissioner for Managing the Affairs of the Austn. Agricl. Compy.
Entd. J. Edward Ebsworth Accountant.

Cheque dated 13th February, 1834, showing signatures of two A.A. Co. Commissioners, Ebsworth & Parry. *Kindly lent by Mr. and Mrs. D. Vyner.*

on "Broomfield" is provided by the collection of stone axeheads picked up on the property in later years. The tribe viewed the new settlers without apparent concern, politely accepting their strange food and stranger customs. They soon learned the value of sheep, "the white man's kangaroos", which they found far easier to catch than their native animals. When the first maize crops ripened in the paddocks, the Aborigines descended like locusts on the rich harvest. When chased away, they took up strategic positions on the hillside and rolled rocks down at their pursuers. Very slowly, the small tribe dwindled.[6]

In 1839, James White purchased "Edinglassie" near Muswellbrook and "Timor Station", twelve miles north of Blandford. It was the same year that Dr. Bowman had taken over "Waverley" estate and "Segenhoe". Dr. Bowman and James White were great friends, often inspecting their properties and various sheep runs together. James White was delighted with the purchase of his property and homestead at "Edinglassie" which he bought from George Forbes, brother of Sir Francis Forbes, first Chief Justice of New South Wales.

The original "Edinglassie" homestead, near Muswellbrook. Built 1833. *Belltrees Library*.

When James White and his family had been at "Edinglassie" three years, James White died in 1842, aged 41, leaving his wife, Sarah, with nine children under the age of 14. Not long after, in 1846, Dr. James Bowman died suddenly. His land and stock were sold and his wife returned to Parramatta to live with her Macarthur family. None of Dr. Bowman's relatives remain today in the Hunter Valley.[7]

By 1848, W. C. Wentworth had become immersed in political, educational and business activities within the colony. James White Junior, then aged 20, leased from Wentworth the "Belltrees" land near his "Broomfield" grant. When his uncle, Edward White, died unmarried in 1850, his mother remained at "Edinglassie" and the "Broomfield" grant became known as "Mrs. White's estate". Later, when Sarah White's sons expanded their interests into the Upper Hunter and, to the ownership of "Broomfield", added "Belltrees", "Ellerston", "Waverley", and key positions in between and when all these properties were converted from leaseland and bought in 1853, they came under the one umbrella of ownership.

The Hon. James White 1828-1890.

CHAPTER FOUR

The White Brothers of "Edinglassie" take over "Belltrees"

FROM 1848, THE CHARACTER OF STATION LIFE at "Belltrees" owed much to the four sons of James White, James, Francis, George and later Henry Charles who assumed control of "Belltrees" after W. C. Wentworth. Of these, James White was the man to whom all brothers turned for advice. He was only fourteen years old when his father died yet his subsequent management knowhow and skill in the selection of the right country stood him in great stead. The runs he selected and developed became leading properties in northern New South Wales. These included "Baroona Station" on the Barwon River; the Narran Lake run, 25 miles away; "Martindale", below the junction of the Hunter and Goulburn Rivers; "Merton" and "Dalswinton" opposite "Martindale"; "Bando Station" in the Liverpool Plains; "Ferridgerie Station" on the Castlereagh River near Coonamble; and later on "Segenhoe" and "Saumarez" — all these were added to "Belltrees", "Ellerston", "Waverley" and "Timor" together with other key runs along the Upper Hunter River between "Ellerston" and "Belltrees". Inevitably, this led to James White becoming a wealthy man, but at the time that he was acquiring new country it was his inherent knowledge and understanding of the land rather than his financial position which secured his success.

But it is not just as a pastoralist that James White made his mark. He became a worthy politician as well.

From December, 1864 to May, 1868 he represented the Hunter District in the Legislative Assembly. He resigned that position in order to travel, and spent four years in England and Europe. It was while he was in London in 1871 that he negotiated the purchase of the famous "Segenhoe" estate for his brother, Francis, and himself. When he returned to Australia he was nominated for the Legislative Council in 1874. Through his association with the architect Horbury Hunt, James White built many magnificent homes and station buildings. In the late 1870's, he rebuilt "Edinglassie" homestead; a 42 stand shearing shed was built on "Belltrees"; the fairy tale "Kirkham", now named "Camelot", near Camden was constructed; and, with his brothers, James White subscribed benevolently to the building of many Churches and Cathedrals (some of them designed by Horbury Hunt) in northern New South Wales. These include Cathedrals at Newcastle and Grafton, St. Alban's Church at Muswellbrook, St. Luke's Church at Scone, St. Paul's at Murrurundi, St. Matthew's at Gundy and the family Chapel, St. James, at "Belltrees". In his later years, the Hon. James White spent much of his time at "Cranbrook", Sydney, and "Kirkham". It was at this stage in his life that he launched himself on a turf career that was to stagger the colony. It was a career which yielded him a fortune and earned him the reputation as one of the fairest owners in the sport. His horses

Chester – 1874-1891. Winner of V.R.C. Derby and Melbourne Cup. *Race Horses in Australia.*

won nearly every major race on the Australian calendar and some of the major events several times. It was a succession of turf victories not since equalled by any owner.

In 1877, Chester, the horse he considered to be his greatest, won the V.R.C. Derby and Melbourne Cup double. James White's betting on the double was such that some of the leading bookmakers were rendered almost bankrupt. Spurred on by this success, he founded the "Kirkham" stud at Camden with the express purpose of producing thoroughbreds. This decision began an extraordinary chapter in Australian racing history and some of James White's horses will remain part of Australia's turf legends. He won the Melbourne Cup twice, the V.R.C. and A.J.C. Derbys four times each; the Maribyrnong Plate twice, and the Australian Cup twice. Within twelve months, his champion Martini Henry won the V.R.C. Derby, the Melbourne Cup, the V.R.C. Sires Produce Stakes and the V.R.C. St. Leger. Another of his champions, Abercorn, was the only horse that could hold the mighty Carbine and three times beat Carbine at weight-for-age.[1] From January, 1878 to April, 1890, sixty of the Hon. James White's horses won 240 races grossing him, in prize money alone, over £121,000, in current values, more than $4 million. Only sickness and eventually his death brought to an end James White's concerted attempt to produce an Australian winnner of the famous English Derby.

James White died in 1890 at the age of 62. Because he had no children, the continuation of the line of Whites at "Belltrees" fell to his brother, Francis. He was born in 1830 and educated at Maitland. He was a quieter man, generally referred to as "Honest Frank White". Like most of his family, he disliked public appearances although he too represented his Upper Hunter District in the Legislative Assembly from 1874 to 1875.

Francis White Esq.
Belltrees Library.

While he helped manage the family stations, in partnership with his brothers, he also believed in helping his local community. He was President of the local Agricultural Society, took an active part in the management of the hospital and the Benevolent Society of Muswellbrook. He was Chairman of the Bench of Magistrates in the district and a great advocate of justice. For example, it annoyed him to think that people in the Upper Hunter region between 1865 and 1870 were actually sheltering the bushranger Thunderbolt and he wrote to the Police Magistrate on at least one occasion to protest against the willingness of locals to harbour the bushranger. At the time, gold was being mined at the Denison diggings nearby and Francis White warned that the path of a witness to any attack was a perilous one indeed; that one of his own workers, Neil McInnes, "was living in great dread of injury to his person or his property . . . that one of (McInnes') horses had come home with a bullet in its shoulder . . . "[2] Tragically, in 1875, Francis White died at "Edinglassie" having caught a fever whilst travelling from "Saumarez" near Armidale, to the Hunter Valley on his way to Sydney for the Opening of Parliament. He was only 45.

Relatively little is known of George White. He came to "Belltrees" in 1848 with his two elder brothers, and in 1860 he married Adelaide Cobb of "Annambah", Maitland. His brother, Francis, had earlier married Adelaide's sister, Mary Hannah Cobb. George White and Adelaide Cobb were married at "Belltrees" but his wife died soon afterwards, and George White moved to "Glen-yr-fron" near Muswellbrook. In 1871, George White married Frances Corinda Bell, and this year, whilst still maintaining a share of the "Belltrees" capital, he relinquished his managerial rights at "Belltrees" to his younger brother, Henry Charles. George White died in the following year aged 41 leaving his interest in "Belltrees" to his new wife.

Although Henry Charles White had been associated with his brothers in other properties for many years, his stake in "Belltrees" only occurred in 1871 when he became a partner with his brothers James and Francis. But by 1875, George and Francis had died and the Hon. James White had become almost exclusively interested in racing, politics and travel. As a result, the management of "Belltrees" was left more and more to the younger brother, Henry Charles.

Following in the footsteps of his brother James, Henry Charles White also employed Horbury Hunt to design buildings for him. In 1875 he built sandstone stables and a workman's cottage at "Glenalvon" and this picturesque property is today owned by my sister-in-law and her husband, Primrose and David Arnott. In 1881, Henry Charles White rebuilt the magnificent "Havilah" homestead.

Mary Hannah White (née Cobb)
Kindly lent by Mr. and Mrs. D. Vyner.

Henry Charles White, Esq.
The Sydney Mail 16.3.1905.

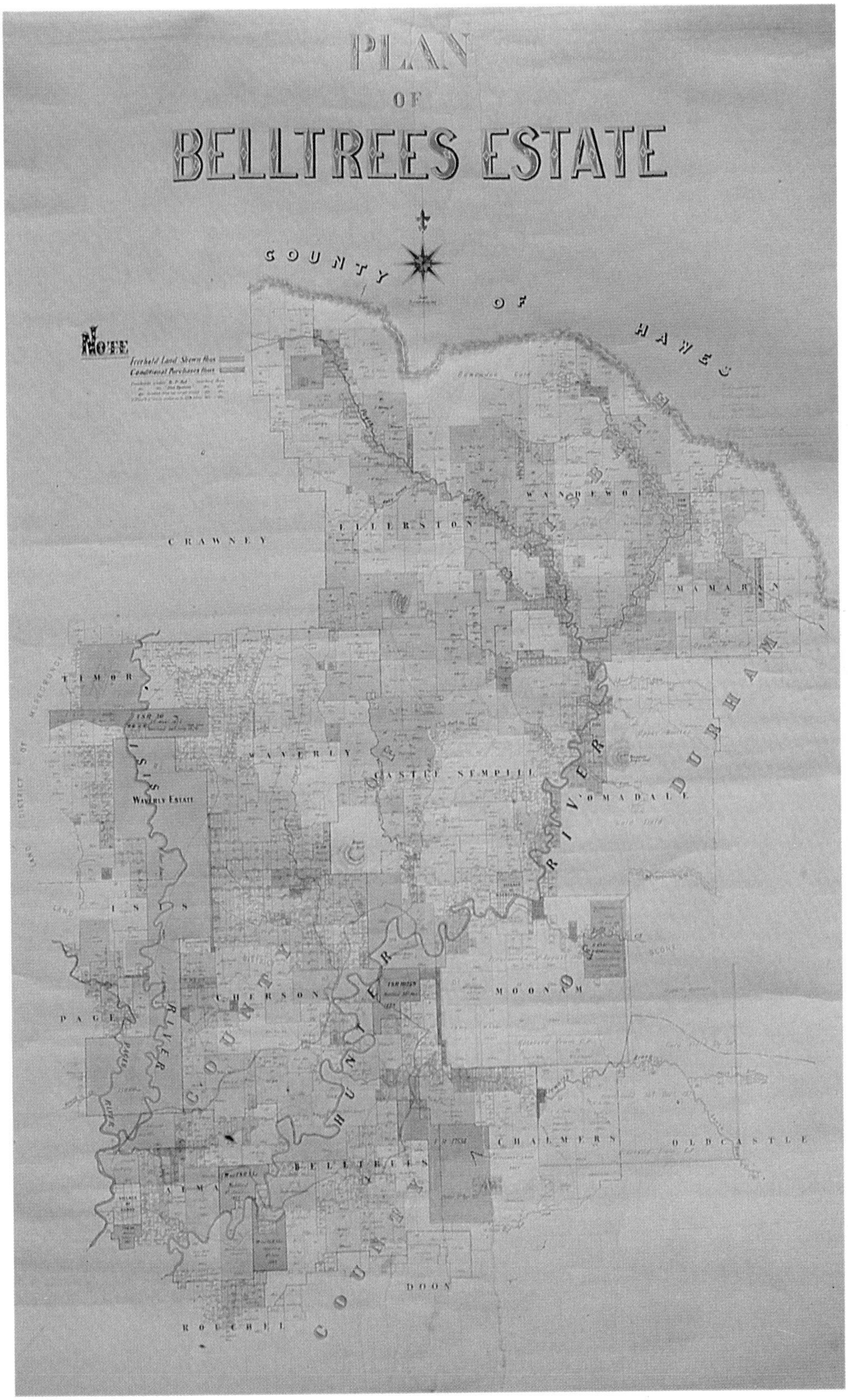

Plan of Belltrees Estate drawn by surveyor H. L. White. *Laurence Le Guay.*

Above: Oil painting of Belltrees by Conrad Martens c. 1862. *Kindly lent by the White family of Saumarez.*

Left: Mustering sheep along the Hunter River flats.
Laurence Le Guay.

Above: View of the shearing shed, built by Horbury Hunt 1876.
Laurence Le Guay.

Right: Detail of hand-blades on shearing shed roof.
Laurence Le Guay.

Running in the stock horses. *Laurence Le Guay.*

Hundreds of miles of post and rail fences were constructed round "Belltrees" in the late 19th Century. *Laurence Le Guay.*

CHAPTER FIVE

Consolidation

THE ACHIEVEMENTS OF THE FOUR BROTHERS at "Belltrees" inspires a genuine respect for their capacity to succeed in the face of significant obstacles. Their father, James White, had died in 1842 at an early age, leaving a wife, seven sons and two daughters. For the next 41 years, four of these sons, James, Francis, George and Henry Charles, either singly or together were in charge at "Belltrees". In 1848 the eldest of them, James, was only 20 but he had the vision, as the opportunity presented itself, to lease the "Belltrees" land from William Charles Wentworth and to purchase it in 1853, and then "Ellerston" in 1854. Along with his brothers, he realised the wool producing potential of the vast Upper Hunter area in general, and "Belltrees" in particular. He inherited the lessons learned by his father who had gained invaluable experience of sheep farming under the most difficult and rugged conditions of the Australian Agricultural Company holding at Stroud. Initially, the brothers lived at "Edinglassie" near Muswellbrook so they understood not only the value of rich river flats but also the potential of the rugged Upper Hunter range land. "Belltrees" possessed both.

The management of such diverse and widespread holdings meant that the brothers rode hundreds of miles over northern New South Wales constantly supervising the musters, the culling and the shearing on their various properties. They developed a keen eye and an acute sense of judgment for new and potentially profitable holdings and bought key positions along the way. They may have been squatters, but they were seldom idle or in one place for long. In an attempt to improve the quality of stock on their various holdings, they embarked on constant movement of herds from one property to another. In this way, "Belltrees" gained from the movement to it of Durham cattle from "Edinglassie"; sheep from "Havilah", and thoroughbred horses from the "Kirkham" stables. At the fountainhead of the family was the eldest of the brothers, James White. All his knowhow, drive and leadership were required during the difficult 1860's.

In these years, borrowing money from the banks was not easy. By the end of the 1860's, two-thirds of the squatting stations in New South Wales were in the hands of the banks and the absence of ready finance meant that many properties became unsaleable and fell into banking interests. But even without this, rural work presented many problems. A new and dreadful disease, pleuro-pneumonia, broke out amongst the cattle and there were heavy losses. As well, large areas remained unfenced and the general muster for such purposes as inoculation or branding required many stockmen and capable, footsure horses. Often the only fenced areas were the horse paddock, the stock yards and the land under cultivation about the homestead. Generally speaking, within a few miles of the homestead, cattle were fairly quiet but further away in the ranges they were wild and difficult to muster.

Many of the horses used in the Upper Hunter were bred by the "A. A". Company at Stroud. They were about fourteen hands, immensely strong and wiry, some a mixture of Arab with English or Australian thoroughbred and even some showing traces of Welsh pony blood. The horses adapted to the work they had to do over the rough terrain but some of the most difficult and dangerous of the stock work lay in rounding up wild horses or brumbies. Many marvellous stories are told about mustering brumbies from the top of Mt. Woolooma. In all these pursuits, the White brothers participated alongside their men — the boss alongside his employees. In this way, knowledge was transmitted. James, Francis and George White involved their younger brother, Henry Charles, in their cattle and sheep musters and often moved the stock from one property to another.

So much of the history of "Belltrees" and other White holdings could only be gleaned from accounts tendered by people who worked on the stations and for the "bosses". In 1863, Robert Donaldson, only 16 years of age, was employed by

Henry Charles White at "Bando". He subsequently wrote, in part, that:

> "... (Henry Charles) was deeply respected by the men who worked for him ... though a pretty stiff task master, under his instructions I learned nearly all I know of the working of stock ... from milking a cow to riding a race. Mr. White was a great lover of horses and a splendid rider. He taught me how to balance in a race and hold a horse together ... I was taught to class sheep ... and I also became a fair expert at counting sheep ... about this time I was sent out with a party of men yardmaking. Four of the men were 'ticket of leave' men and the stories they told of their old convict days were startling ..."[1]

Something of the tyranny of distance is captured in another of Donaldson's stories concerned with the birth of one of Mr. White's children.

> ". . . the overseer was dispatched for a doctor 50 miles away. On arrival there, he found the doctor had died two days previously, so he turned and rode the 50 miles back, doing 100 miles in ten hours on the same horse. I heard him say if necessary the horse would have carried him another 50 miles . . . in the meantime my mother had been sent to attend Mrs. White, when another little daughter was born, and everything went well . . ."[2]

(This daughter named Marion Cecil subsequently became the wife of G. M. Mathews, the famous ornithologist and confidant of H. L. White.)

Donaldson also recalls changes in management that came about as the White interest in "Belltrees" quickened:

> ". . . soon after . . . changes were made in the management, Mr. White going to another of the firm's properties 'Belltrees' in the Upper Hunter . . . I went to 'Belltrees' with Mr. White; also my sister who had been with the family as a sort of confidential nurse, went with them and remained with the White family until the death of Mrs. White at the birth of another child, a son in 1875 . . ."[3]

The primitiveness and privation of outback Australia is recalled by Donaldson in the same account:

> ". . . during my stay at 'Belltrees', about two years, mostly working amongst cattle and horses, I had some adventures. When riding through the paddocks I came across a man, stark naked, sitting on a log. It was a blazing hot day and the unfortunate man was almost roasted. I rode home and reported and men were sent to bring him in, but he had cleared out in the meantime. . . . he was one of the shepherds who had gone insane, left his sheep and roamed some days before I saw him. About two years later I was about to drive sheep from Belltrees' to 'Bando'; this same man was engaged as one of the drovers . . ."[4]

Mr. Robert Donaldson (c. 1900).
Kindly lent by Mr. R. Hawkins.

Through Mr. Donaldson's tales we understand the problems faced by men who were left alone to struggle with the disasters of the silent bush.

> ". . . on another occasion on 'Belltrees' when out riding up a creek I met a man riding a splendid looking horse; a fine looking chap, fairly well dressed. He stopped and spoke asking me who I was and where from. I told him and asked if he was one of the Mr. Carters who had a neighbouring station. He said, no, but was in a hurry. Good morning boy, he said, as he galloped off. He was the notorious Fred Ward, otherwise called Captain Thunderbolt."[5]

These pictorial accounts and reminiscences are invaluable and give an idea of life on a property in the latter part of the last century. It is sometimes difficult to live on an estate in modern times and visualise the way of life one hundred years ago. Even the notion of densely-timbered, unfenced lands defies total belief. There are, however, some features which do remain unchanged. In the 1860's men remarked on being wakened in the morning by the sound of wild birds.

> "About the orchard and garden hundreds of magpies assembled and poured forth their remarkable and beautiful carols. The small pigeon magpies with their more shrill notes and a few laughing jackasses and butcher birds added to the music; but the noisiest of all were the domestic guinea fowls. Frugivorous birds were so numerous it was almost impossible to obtain ripe fruit from the orchard . . ."[6]

The songs of native birds still remain at "Belltrees", an emblem of the Australian bush, a natural link with the past which has undergone great change.

By 1885, the Hon. James and Henry Charles White were tired of their managerial responsibilities. Willingly they delegated the task of management to their nephew Henry Luke White, son of Francis White. The advent of documented "Belltrees" history now begins. For, from the first instance that Henry Luke White accepted his responsible position, he entered all accounts into diaries or letter form. He wrote frequently to his Uncle James and Uncle Henry until he was able to feel confident enough to transfer his interest from other family properties and purchase "Belltrees" in his own right. One such lengthy piece of correspondence merits, in part, reproduction. (See also Appendix II). It is a letter written early in 1888 by Henry Luke White to his Uncle, the Hon. James White, then residing in Sydney.

> "My dear Uncle,
>
> I enclose you a return of the permanent hands on 'Belltrees', 'Ellerston' and 'Waverley' and the wages they receive. I cannot see

Conrad Martens sketches of "Belltrees – The seat of Francis White Esq." 1862.
Courtesy of Mitchell Library and Dixson Gallery.

how we are to do with any less . . . there are forty hands employed, of these sixteen are boundary riders who have over 350 miles of fencing to look after; an average of over 20 miles per man. I think these boundary riders are very necessary, and if it is worthwhile putting up fences it is surely worthwhile keeping them in repair. We have about ten sheep musterers who are men knowing every inch of the different paddocks; temporary men would not do the work nearly so well nor could they be of value just when they were wanted most. The sheep musterers have been at their work every day almost, since last July; after this week they will have to go burr cutting till the rams have to be taken from the ewes, then all the sale ewes have to be mustered and sent to 'Bando'. I suppose men of this sort are not to be had at a minute's notice; and those you could get would ask higher wages and are not worth their salt. Paddocks in this country are not easily mustered, one of our large paddocks takes five men three days to clean up; some of the 'Ellerston' ones are still worse. Stockmen when not employed with cattle help with the sheep. They are fully employed now in moving cattle about into different sheep paddocks to try and keep grass seed down. I cannot see how any reduction can be made in the permanent staff of men. I put the enormous expense down to pear cutting, and think you will find that in another six or eight months that will be all over. It was 'penny wise and pound foolish' policy not going into them years ago, when they were comparatively thin. I have now two paddocks of scattered pears and three thick patches of about fifty acres each to do. After these are down, five or six good men should be able to keep all the ground ones down . . ."[7]

Henry Luke's father died at an early age giving H. L. White an immediate insight into the problems of administration and the need for decisive decision making. This account shows not just a complete understanding of the detail of management but also it demonstrates a maturity and sense of discipline necessary for making management effective. The same letter highlights the fact that H. L. White had inherited his uncle's instinct for taking up good land when it became available:

". . . W. S. Baker, the man who tendered so high for the land on Stewart's Brook and got it, has thrown his lease up; as he cannot afford to pay the money for it, the land (1,370 acres) is now up for lease. I think we should have another try to get it. Baker has retained and fenced some of the other leases in so that one line of fence would make a paddock of the lease in question. . . ."[8]

The letter ends with an explicit answer to the question of cost which obviously provoked such a detailed reply to his uncle:

". . . I shall attend to what you say about paying the men at the end of the quarter only. The amount paid to pear cutters last year was £1,206/11/3.

Your affectionate nephew,
Henry L. White."[9]

In current values this amount paid to pear cutters is equivalent to over $44,000.

As the involvement of Henry Luke White strengthened in "Belltrees", it was inevitable that before long he would, with the assistance of his brothers Ernest, Arthur and Victor, seek outright ownership including the "Waverley" and "Ellerston" estates.

To achieve this, the partnership of the Hon. James, Francis and Henry Charles White had to be dissolved and realised; and in order to purchase "Belltrees", the interests held by the four sons of Francis White in "Edinglassie", "Bando", "Segenhoe" and "Saumarez" would have to be surrendered.

As I have already pointed out, the Hon. James White had no children and his interests were now increasingly concentrated in Sydney. The interests of Henry Charles White were already absorbed in "Havilah", "Bando", "Woodlands" and "Wallon" stations and later he chose to reside at "Greenoaks", now "Bishopscourt", Darling Point. All this simplified the move towards the ownership of "Belltrees" by Francis White's four sons, Henry Luke, Ernest, Arthur and Victor. But there were six sons in this family. The eldest of the boys, Francis John went to "Saumarez" and there founded the New England branch of the White family. The second son, James Cobb White, remained at "Edinglassie". The four youngest boys, Henry Luke, Ernest, Arthur and Victor went to "Belltrees".

By October 25, 1889, the final transactions were tabled thus:

- "Belltrees" was valued at £244,253, over $8 million in current values.
- "Bando" which went to Henry Charles White and the Cobb family, was valued at £155,500, in current values over $5 million.
- "Saumarez" was valued at £24,750 or nearly $1 million.
- "Edinglassie" was valued at £52,000 or in current values $1¾ million.
- "Segenhoe" was sold to the Land Company of Australia Limited for £56,573, in current values almost $2 million.[10]

This left the four brothers on "Belltrees" in default of £20,000 ($680,000 in current values) which they borrowed from their

Group of "Belltrees" shearers 1880, using handblades. *Belltrees Library.*

Bale of W.W.W. wool. *H. L. White.*

Interior of "Belltrees" 42-stand shearing shed. *Wesley Stacey*.

uncles the Hon. James and Henry Charles White. This enabled the sons to provide an annuity for Mrs. George White and an income for their mother, Mrs. Francis White, and their sister, Mary Grigson. Consistent with what is understood of the uncles, not only did they assist financially but also they were ever ready with advice.

The Hon. James White died in 1890 but Henry Charles continued to help the firm. Even when he moved to Sydney to pursue his interests, Henry Charles White was still a tower of strength and enjoyed horse racing with his nephews. He died in Sydney in 1905 and by then the firm H. E. A. & V. White stood on its own merit.

Belltrees stud ewes (c. 1900). Photo shows the "White cottage", with adjoining "single fellows" quarters in background. *Courtesy Scone Historical Society.*

CHAPTER SIX

The Partnership

THE PARTNERSHIP H. E. A. & V. WHITE, in control of "Belltrees" from 1889, began a period of prosperity and achievement that saw the property scale new heights as a rural enterprise. The management, expertise and resources of "Belltrees" during this period enabled it to withstand the effects of great local, national and international crises. It is a complex period, and this chapter seeks to isolate some of the influences on, and challenges facing the management at "Belltrees" during this time. The partnership brought together, above all else, a complementarity of interests involving the four brothers, Henry Luke, Ernest, Arthur and Victor.

One of the strengths of Victor, the youngest brother, was his capacity to enjoy life on the station and to see the point of view of the men who worked there. He had three elder brothers who enjoyed giving orders and Victor was happy to play his role in a lower key. In fact, he idolised racing and would have much preferred being at the racetrack, rather than mustering in a paddock or working in the yards. In 1907, he put it to his elder brothers that they could manage in his absence, and he indicated a desire to pull out of the partnership. This would have meant realising on his share of the property and would have involved selling large tracts of "Belltrees". Victor generously agreed to remain within the partnership and did not withdraw his interests until 1936.

In 1910, at the age of 42, he married Ruth Withycombe, went for a trip to England and then moved to Sydney to live. Earlier, three Ebsworth sisters had married Victor's brothers - James Cobb White of "Edinglassie" and Henry Luke and Arthur of "Belltrees". These sisters were indeed formidable. Bill Smith, the gardener who left "Belltrees" in 1926 and went to work with Mr. and Mrs. Victor White at "Lulworth" in Darlinghurst, Sydney, told me, "that the combination of the three Ebsworth sisters was just too strong for Mrs. Victor".

In 1912 a son was born to the Victor Whites and they named him Patrick. In 1925, Victor White travelled to England and put his son to school. Henry Luke White subsequently wrote to Victor in England with a sense of the future of which he was certainly unconscious at the time:

> "I note you have put Patrick to school, where I hope he will make a name for himself; from all accounts the boy has plenty of brains ...[1]"

"H. L." was always interested in his nephew's scholarly progress. If H. L. White had been alive in 1973, how proud he would have been of this talented nephew when Patrick Martindale White won the Nobel Prize for Literature, the first Australian to do so.

Alec Wiseman, who is still at "Belltrees" today after more than fifty years of service, described A. G. White, the third of the four brothers, as "Nature's gentleman". "A. G." as he was affectionately known, was a calm and co-operative man who accepted as unchallengeable the leadership of H. L. White. Arthur White was a popular man, who understood the men in his charge and their work and, in return, the men respected his discipline. Above all, he was a generous, philanthropic man. Elsewhere, in this chapter, I have indicated his contribution to Australia's war effort. He and his brother Victor were Foundation Donors to the Cranbrook School, and The King's School, Parramatta, benefited greatly from the bequest of Arthur White. In 1924, he purchased 92 acres of Bakewell's paddock, Scone, and gave it to the people of Scone. Today, known as "White Park", it is the scene of a golf course, a race track, cricket field and a rodeo ground. Arthur also financed the building of the Scone Scout Hall; and it was his underwriting that enabled Scone to be lit by electricity. In his later years, following the death of his brother Henry Luke, he left "Belltrees" and lived in Sydney at the Hotel Australia with his wife, while retaining a 50% interest in the property until he died in 1948.

The second son in the partnership, Ernest White, never married. He was a brilliant horseman. Whenever any stockman or brother had a good horse, everyone knew that Ernest would commandeer it sooner or later. His horses were fit and Ernest

The six sons of Francis White:
Seated: James Cobb White, Francis John White, Henry Luke White.
Standing: Victor Martindale White, Arthur George White
and William Ernest White. *"Belltrees" 22.4.1913.*

travelled so far each day that his dogs were often unable to keep up with him. To prove the fitness of him and his horse, each evening Ernest, after a fifty mile ride, would return and jump his horse over the fence into the horse yard. He played polo and rode numerous winners in picnic races and was, in fact, still riding at picnics at the age of 45, only four years before he died. He was essentially a man of the turf and when he died in 1914, aged 49, the flag at Moorefield Racetrack was flown at halfmast in his honour.[2]

There can be no doubt that at the helm of the H. E. A. & V. White partnership for almost forty years was Henry Luke White, known as "H. L.".

He was born at "Annambah", Maitland, in 1860. The story is told that the night before he was born, his mother, Mary, drove to Maitland in a sulky with her brother. On the way, so the story goes, the reins broke and the horse bolted. The brother was terrified for his sister who calmly climbed over the front seat and let herself fall into a good patch of soft grass. That night H. L. White was born. This provoked the comment that "H. L." had a good start in life with such a sensible mother.[3]

There is no doubt that H. L. White grew up to be a highly principled, intensely nationalistic individual who viewed everything he did on a grand scale. His philosophy of achievement and perfection did not apply to the property "Belltrees" alone. He fulfilled his ambition to build up two invaluable national collections, one of birds' eggs and skins and one of postage stamps; and he applied himself wholeheartedly in local community affairs. He was President of the Scone Shire Council from 1906 to 1927, which, at the time, was a State record. During this time he missed only two meetings and that was when flood waters prevented his journey through river crossings between "Belltrees" and Scone. He was determined to have a dry road along the Upper Hunter reaches and doggedly hammered away through Government departmental channels until his objective became a reality. His "firm" commenced the movement by donating the "White Bridge" to the Shire and then backing the construction of the project. The elimination of river crossings facilitated the transport of wool, wheat crops and stock from the head of the Hunter into the Scone railhead and other markets.

"H. L." was always interested in the work of the Upper Hunter Pastures Protection Board. He was a member of the Board from 1886 to 1921 and part of that time he spent as Chairman. In 1919, "H. L." and his two elder brothers headed the Pastures Protection Board polls in their respective districts — Francis J. White of "Saumarez" in Armidale; the Hon. James Cobb White of

Top: Mail coach crossing a stream of liquid mud (8.12.1919). H. L. White pledged himself to create a dry road for the Upper Hunter Valley. *H. L. White.*

Bottom: Pulling a Chevrolet car out of Bell's Crossing of the Hunter River. *H. L. White.*

"Edinglassie" at Denman, and "H. L." of "Belltrees" in Scone. A newspaper at the time remarked,

> "The voting, besides being a unique record, is striking evidence of the popularity of the White family amongst stock owners. It speaks volumes of their services to the industry — the industry which their stock and money and brains and enterprise have helped to develop. It is good to see good men in the livestock industry appreciated by their fellow stock owners."[4]

Victor White

While H. L. White allocated large amounts of his time to community affairs, the expansion at "Belltrees" continued. By the end of the nineteenth century it had become a little settlement. Not only did the station provide employment for the men, but also it was responsible for the community life as a whole, providing education, entertainment and a place from which to buy one's provisions. "Belltrees" and "Ellerston" were virtually two little colonies working in conjunction.

At this stage there were about 62 buildings listed for valuation on the "Belltrees" estate. Apart from the main homestead, there were stables, a Church, entertainment halls and engine sheds, 18 boundary riders' houses, three drovers' huts and 18 other residences belonging to farmers, gardeners, managers and bookkeepers. There were many families and about 250 permanent residents not including temporary labour. Inevitably, schools were set up at both "Ellerston" and "Belltrees" to educate the children. As early as 1867, William Isaac was registered as a teacher at "Ellerston". Before long, the Council of Education granted "Belltrees" provisional school status and a teacher, Mr. Allen, formally took charge there on May 1, 1876.[5] By 1882, there were 48 pupils at the school; and by 1891 "Ellerston" provisional school recorded twenty pupils from the Fermor, Tilse, McNamara, Hines, Pinkerton and Taylor families.[6] These families also appear in the documented records of the "Ellerston" store book of 1894 which contains some interesting debit entries. Apart from anything else, these give an impressive insight into costs at the time, for example:

Jas. Pinkerton	10 lb. beef	2/1p.
G. F. Cobb	1 pair strong boots	10/6p.
F. G. Hayne	14 lb. of nails	3/6p.
Granny Taylor	1 set horseshoes & nails	1/3p.
W. Tilse	6 yards of calico	2/6p.
J. Mitchell	1 pair of boots	8/6p.
W. Quinn	20 lb. of flour	2/6p.
G. F. Rosington	2 x 5/8 brace bits	3/4p.[7]

Arthur White

Ernest White

"One day at the 'Belltrees' school, the Clergyman was giving a Divinity lesson. 'Who made the world?' he asked the children. One small boy put up his hand. 'Please Sir, Mr. H. L. White.' "

The answer was perhaps unexpected but nonetheless heartfelt. For as head of "Belltrees" community, H. L. White always felt responsible for each family's well being. He was a very organised man, and every morning "the boss" gave orders to his men and knew exactly where and when to find them throughout the day. He knew how much work a man could do within a certain time. He treated his workers well, showed great leadership of them and was admired by them. He was often abrupt but he expected decisiveness and commitment from his men and in return they could expect fairness from him.

To the employees' wives, H. L. White let it be known that if a child was injured or sick, or immediate help was needed, they could call on him any hour of the day or night. He was willing to give advice and would lend money if he thought the cause just. While he upheld the philosophy that "He helps those who help themselves", H. L. White never failed to back a good worker.

The "Belltrees" ironbark slab store was a familiar meeting place for the workers. Bullock-drawn, and later horse-drawn waggons would arrive there from Morpeth and Newcastle laden with goods, fencing material and all manner of provisions from D. Cohen & Company, the merchants of Newcastle. D. Cohen & Company did much to assist the farmer in good times and bad. They allowed credit in time of drought and they knew that accounts would be settled when the wool cheques arrived. This same slab store still stands today at the bottom of the homestead garden. It was built by H. C. Sempill in 1836. It was also the place where the mail coach brought the morning mail bag. In the early part of the century, the horse-drawn coach would leave the Scone Post Office at 7 a.m. and arrive at "Belltrees" at 11.30 a.m. — a journey of four-and-a-half hours through many river crossings. Today the trip by the motor mail van is a half-hour drive on a dry road. The same van continues up the Valley to Moonan and "Ellerston", twenty-five miles away. In those days, the horse-drawn Moonan coach would meet the Scone mail coach at the "Belltrees" slab store and goods would be transferred from one coach to the other.

Henry Luke White

Mr. Viger's mail coach leaving Scone post office. c. 1915.
Courtesy Scone Historical Society.

H. L. White was a stickler for time. It's often recalled that if a client was five minutes late any deal previously negotiated with "H. L." was off. The extent to which this pre-occupation with exact time often passed into unacceptable eccentricity is indicated by the fact that "H. L." would record how long it took the Scone mail coach to turn around, change horses, and return to Scone. If the mailman "yarned", the Scone office would be informed.

At all times, "H. L." and his brothers, Ernest, Arthur and Victor operated as a team in the management of "Belltrees". Together they embarked on projects — acquiring extra land, increasing stock levels and implementing wideranging improvements to the property. "H. L." was "the boss" — the sheepman; Ernest, the expert on horses and cattle; "A. G." supervised the men and the work-gangs doing fencing, scrub cutting, pearing, etc., and Victor co-operated wherever he was needed demonstrating a great capacity to keep the operations running smoothly. Any decision that had to be taken was made by the four partners together. If one brother was overseas, which often occurred, no agreement was reached until each member of "the firm" granted approval. The network was a close one. "H. L." seldom left "Belltrees" but if Arthur and Victor were away he wrote to them with daily accounts of station life.

Top: Stacking iron bark fence posts at "Belltrees". Feb. 1925. *H. L. White.*
Bottom: Pit-sawing timber in the bush at "Belltrees". Jan 1923. *H. L. White.*

"Belltrees" and its operations in 1889, the firm immediately felt the impact of one of the worst droughts in recorded history. In 1888, the station experienced only 11.89 inches of rain, well below the expected average of more than 26 inches. In fact, the vagaries of rural life are recorded in duplicate in every letter that H. L. White wrote. By reading them, one could be forgiven for imagining that life on the land was no more than an endurance of droughts, fires, pests and floods. Few references are made to the profitable sales of cattle, sheep and wool which balanced the scales and enabled "Belltrees" to withstand profound seasonal variations.

Interesting facts emerge from the letters and the records of H. L. White. In 1902, when only 19 inches of rain were recorded on the property, for the first time in its history, cattle were sent away from "Belltrees". "H. L.'s" records show that one thousand head were agisted and five hundred died; that shearing was postponed because all the lambs had died; and that when the rains did fall in October, one thousand strong, newly shorn wethers were killed bringing to four thousand the total number of sheep that were lost.

While seasonal conditions improved slightly, the political atmosphere became increasingly gloomy for the man on the land. The Federal Government in 1911 threatened land owners with a Land Tax. "H. L." consulted his elder brother James Cobb White of "Edinglassie", as both men were worried about the impending Tax and closer settlement problems. In early 1911, H. L. White decided to sell "Belltrees". He wrote to the Chairman of the Closer Settlement Advisory Board in Tamworth with the news that,

> "We have now decided to offer you the whole of our Belltrees estate, less about 10,000 acres around the homestead and two outlying blocks containing 3,000 acres. The area offered you is about 140,000 acres . . . Our price is £3 per acre all round. The above offer is subject to the approval of one member of our firm (V. M. White) who is abroad at present, but whose consent will be a matter of course only . . ."[8]

Fortunately, the sale did not eventuate. It must have been a daunting figure for the Board to agree to — £420,000, in current background to the purchase of "Terreel":

> ". . . We were compelled to send cattle away from Belltrees to save the lives of our breeders and young stock. After reaching the Stroud district, where the best feed was to be found at the time, and finding no suitable agistment country, we were forced to purchase Terreel which carried a fine coat of grass on the improved portion. In view of the recognised value of grazing land in proportion to the stock carrying capability . . . we paid considerably more than the property was worth. Calculating six sheep as being equal to one head of large stock and the carrying capacity of Terreel being one thousand head of cattle, the value should not be more than 30 shillings per acre. At the time of purchase we were very hard pressed for relief country and were compelled to purchase at any price. A personal inspection by two members of 'the firm' was made . . ."[9]

Having thus overcome the problem of drought relief, "H. L." was still dubious about his relationship with the Taxation Commissioner on the question of property improvement. He wrote to the Deputy Commissioner of Taxation in Sydney in August, 1912 listing the "value of improvements upon the Belltrees estate" as:

Fencing	£30,000
Clearing scrub, etc.	£30,000
Ringbarking, suckering, etc.	£49,000
Buildings	£38,000
Water conservation	£ 2,000
Cultivation and clearing	£10,000
Yards	£ 2,000
Roads, bridges and telephones	£ 2,000
	£163,000[10]

In current values, more than $5 million.

The extent of these improvements gives some indication of the size and managerial demands of "Belltrees" then. Nevertheless, from July 1, 1913 to October 31, 1914 "the firm" sold more than 5,700 head of cattle for £52,000, in current money terms approximately $1.7 million. Against this it must be said that, in order to save grass, "H. L." of necessity had 21,000 kangaroos destroyed.

It was demands such as this that made H. L. White increasingly tired of his task and he wrote in June 1913 to his egg collector, Whitlock, in Western Australia expressing a view similar to the one of only two years ago which he offered to the Closer Settlement Advisory Board. In part, he said,

> ". . . I wish I could get rid of this place at a decent price. I am tired of the worry of management. The trouble is that it is too big for anyone except the Government."[11]

He even tried to tempt the Government with a portion of the place by offering them 60,000 acres at "Ellerston" but this offer was rejected. He sought to lighten his load by selling some of his grants along the Upper Hunter River and in 1914 sold "Waverley" station to the Payne brothers of "Wombramurra", Nundle.

But "H. L." suffered a deep personal blow in 1914, when Ernest died suddently of appendicitis in Sydney. "H. L." had relied so much on him. It was he who left the station each morning riding either to "Waverley" or "Ellerston" and returning home in the evening to report to "the boss" on the condition of the cattle, sheep, fences and country. His presence at "Belltrees" was taken for granted. Like all capable men, his work was only truly realised when he was gone. The sale of "Waverley" was a major step by H. L. White as "Waverley" station was the portion of "Belltrees" that his brother Ernest had organised to own as his separate property. Its sale was a manifestation of the grief that "H. L." felt at Ernest's death. But by 1915 "H. L.'s" optimism had returned and he wrote,

> ". . . Our season continues first rate, cattle fattening fast, I never experienced a better summer . . ."

The evidence of "H. L.'s" correspondence points to the validity of this statement. During 1915, "the firm" had disposed of 40,000 acres of land and prided itself on not selling one beast in store condition. But there were still plagues of blow-flies, blowing the rams around the heads and the young ewes at the top of the shoulders. And there was no cheap, reliable cure. Then, in 1916 there was a new pest, "the procession caterpillar" which destroyed the acacia and yarran trees; and later, in September of that year a flying fox plague descended in millions upon the property.

Despite all these trials, "H. L." was delighted with his wool

Victor White working at the dehorning bail of stockyards 1901. *Belltrees Library*.

clip in 1916. From 26,000 sheep, only part of the flock, he produced 660 bales of wool, as he said, "the best clip we have ever had". To celebrate, he purchased 950 "Havilah" rams and boasted in November that 12,000 of his wethers had cut 12 pounds of wool per head. But by 1917 things were again, according to "H. L.'s" letters,

> "worse than at any time since 1888; and very few of our visiting birds have, as yet, turned up. Late rain has again caused great mortality amongst the newly-shorn sheep . . . we have lost 1,500 head and ten men have been employed for three days burning carcasses . . . "

The story of 1918 is much the same for, according to "H. L.",

> "Too much rain up to the end of January, then nothing at all, very dry here, a plague of grasshoppers; the brutes clean away every vestige of feed in their track . . . between here and Scone gradually advancing this way, the swarm fills the River valley in width, and is six miles long. The insects being thicker than a swarm of bees . . . a farmer down the River had 50 acres of lucerne seed cleared off in nine hours; so we are racing our fat cattle to market to escape hoppers and price fixers."[12]

One of "H. L.'s" main concerns was that the drought was having a disastrous effect on the native birds that were dying from eating too many pepper berries. He was also concerned that other birds were eating his fruit from the orchard and were attacking the fish which were trapped as the River was drying up. The adverse seasonal conditions were taking their toll of the bird life and this sometimes appeared to depress "the boss" most of all. But, despite the numerous setbacks, "Belltrees" was regarded as a prosperous pastoral establishment, though "H. L." was modest about his achievements. In answer to a request from the Premier's Department in 1918 "H. L." wrote,

> "You have formed quite an erroneous idea of Belltrees which cannot, by any stretch of the imagination, be called a showplace; it is just an ordinary sheep and cattle station with perhaps a little more money spent upon improvements than is usual."[13]

The diaries of this period continue to record in detail the prizes and pitfalls of an increasingly complex rural community. In particular the correspondence of 1924 records that,

> "Pests in force — small flies a record; blow flies in millions; big, brown moths mess all ceilings and walls; cut worms which spoilt our cotton crop, a small stinging fly which sucks the juice of fruit and vegetables has completely destroyed all peaches, figs, mulberries and now into the irrigated maize . . ."[14]

Just seek the rainbow through the storm
Your joys will come again."

I felt sure that "H. L.'s" son, A. H. White, had stuck this verse there to elevate his spirits after having read the desperate accounts of the drought and pests — to lift one's heart, so to speak, as it lifted mine.

As I have said before, so much of the history of "Belltrees" is clarified by the recollections of employees who worked on the property. Mark Lee, of Bell's Creek, has recalled many incidents although he was only on "Belltrees" for two years and two months having had to leave after, as he termed it, "a terrible buster off a horse". He came to "Belltrees" in 1914 when he was only 16 and he remembers,

> ". . . at Belltrees they were shearing 185,000 for those two years and to give you an idea of conditions there were nine stockmen, two farmers, two gardeners, three bullock waggons, carpenters, horse breakers, grooms, a horse trainer for races held after shearing. This was held at the back of the shearing sheds, and that night a great ball to finish the shearing season. . . ."[15]

Tobacco was a big item for the workers and Mark Lee recalls it merging as part of the social scene:

> ". . . the Miss Whites usually gave four smoke concerts each year at the back of the homestead. Cigars, cigarettes, lollies, fruit and fruitcake and tea. All were invited and if you did not attend they would want to know why. . . ."[16]

Mark Lee also records that,

> ". . . when I left 'Belltrees', I left a happy home . . . it was at 'Belltrees' at Sunday school, that Mrs. Lee and I first met, and saw love in each other's eyes . . ."[17]

Such a straightforward and unselfconscious touch adds an important humanity to an obviously difficult environment, where the fight to be successful had to be unrelenting.

the men were constantly lopping trees,

> "At first they made the mistake of only lopping oak trees and killed many cattle, but then when fed with apple tree and oak, the cattle did very well. Even prickly pears were boiled and mixed with pollard and bran to feed the cattle."[19]

After the drought, he remembers heavy falls of snow and later heavy falls of coastal rain occurring each year until 1914 and then another drought lasting four years. Mark Lee was particularly saddened that the River dried up and the fish introduced by Mr. H. L. White were stranded in hot waterholes and eaten by cormorants. Mr. Lee was fascinated that "H. L." had a special train come from Melbourne with trout fingerlings packed on ice, to be liberated into the Hunter River near the old horse yards at "Belltrees". When the streams were running freely he remembers there would be forty or fifty camps fishing along the banks, but after the drought they disappeared.

Mr. Lee's father-in-law, Mr. Thomas Smith, had, back in the 1830's, leased a farm from "Belltrees" on the Stewart's Brook, and Mark Lee remembers that,

> ". . . Mr. Smith grew melons . . . Aborigines would come onto his farm and point to the melons and place their fingers in their mouths, indicating they wanted a feed of melons. Mr. Smith would pick a big feed of them, and they would sit and eat these, and then go away and not be seen till the same time next year . . ."[20]

The paddock leased by Mr. Smith is still called "Smith's" and many paddocks on "Belltrees" bear the name and memory of early settlers — Haynes, Mitchell, McNamara, Sempill, McPhee, Joe Taylor and Garland. It is an omission in our recorded history that there is not a map which indicates the homes which these settlers had in their paddocks.

The most dominant and disturbing feature of the H. L. White era at "Belltrees" was the onset and course of World War I. Though too old to go to the War himself, "H. L." saw that no concerns regarding the War.

> "The War looks worse for us as time goes on, but we live in hope; up to date Australia has enrolled 100,000 men, 75,000 of whom have been sent away fully armed and equipped; considering the class of our politicians, the mixed nationality of the population and our immense distances, I think we have done very well. From our small community just around Belltrees, we have sent more than 50 of our best men. What an awful bungle was made of the early Dardanelles business; with decent management, we should have held possession by now . . ."[21]

'H. L." was proud of all the men who joined from the nearby district, as enlistment was not compulsory. To each recruit he gave a gold watch and took out a life insurance policy in their name. In April, 1916, he ordered watches from Mr. W. Kerr, Watchmaker of George Street, Sydney, and had them especially inscribed for the following men:

> James Mychael, Frank Collison, H. Cobb, James Hillier, R. M. Doyle, James Morrison, A. McInnes, F. A. James, John C. Webeck, Alvar Wilan, Percy Riley, F. G. Ninness, James McGregor, George Morrison, E. H. Cone, Donald Geary, Richard Simpson, Herbert Hillier, W. H. McPhee, Harold Tilse, Thomas Quinn, S. F. Dunbar, and C. Cone.

Amongst the men who enlisted was Arch McInnes, better known as "Bung". He worked as a stockman on "Belltrees", and was famous for his rough riding ability. He joined the nearby Moonan Troop of the Australian Light Horse. He was sent to Egypt and fought in the Sinai Peninsula. During one particular campaign, his Commanding Officer called for a volunteer to ride to the brow of a hill and see how many Turks were on the other side. "I suppose that's what a man is here for," "Bung" was heard to say, and promptly volunteered. He rode to the crest of the hill, stood in his stirrups, hand on the neck of his horse, and looked over the ridge. Bullets came in all directions, incredibly missing "Bung's" head. He galloped back to his C. O., "They're there in bloody thousands," was his report.

"Bung's" brother Neil tried to enlist and was rejected for poor eyesight. He was furious because his friend, James McGregor had

During the War, H. L. White took out War Bonds for some "Belltrees" employees and A.M.P. insurance policies for the employee soldiers fighting at the front, such as Greer, McGeorge, Roe, Doran, Haslam, Tilse, O'Connell, Irving, Crewe, Kitching and Shaw.

One of "H. L.'s" letters is indicative of the pride he felt for the "Belltrees" men.

> ". . . What a wonderful difference there is in men who went to the front. One stockman came back as a colonel with all sorts of honours. Another stockman of ours became a Captain, married a real life Countess in England, and is now managing a rubber

Country voluntary workers camped at Sydney Cricket Ground during 1917 strike.

yet the four White brothers subscribed substantially to the seven War Loans — A. G. White, £143,000, in current money value $3.5 million; H. L. White, £38,000 or $942,400; V. M. White £30,000 or $744,000. "H. L." was furious when the seventh War Loan of October 1918 was unable to be filled. One of his letters reaches a stridency in his condemnation:

> ". . . New South Wales is scratching along trying to make up the seventh War Loan, whilst 75,000 turned up at Randwick Races on Saturday to see Desert Gold beaten and put £100,000 through the tote."[23]

He was also angry that other charities were seeking assistance when the War should have been first priority. The Dean of Newcastle was, on one occasion, the recipient of "H. L.'s" wrath:

> ". . . We are now in the midst of the greatest War ever known in history, and suffering from the worst industrial upheaval ever experienced in New South Wales, yet you ask for substantial contributions to a fund (Newcastle Cathedral Building Fund) which can very well wait until our national troubles are over."[24]

"H. L." was certainly entitled to answer in such a manner as the White family had already been most generous benefactors to the Church of England in New South Wales.

In 1917, during the course of the War, 100,000 men were put off work in New South Wales because of the coal and rail strike. There was rioting, almost civil war. "Belltrees" sent 50 men, 46 horses and an extra 17 saddles to the R. A. S. Showground to help the Mounted Police control the street traffic, and "the firm" sent financial assistance to the New South Wales Government. H. L. White complimented the Acting Premier, Mr. Fuller, on his strong attitude taken in getting voluntary labour to man the mines. Seven thousand country people joined the voluntary work force in Sydney and two hundred went from this district. Some camped at the Cricket Ground. "H. L." outlined the position to Mr. Whitlock, one of his egg collectors in Western Australia, to whom he wrote frequently.

> "Our big strike continues and, to outward appearance, is a long way from settlement; the Railway trouble (the original cause of all

Top: New South Wales No. 1. "The White Belltrees", presented August 17, 1916 by Messrs. H. E. A. & V. White, "Belltrees", Scone. *C. A. Baker.*

Bottom: New South Wales No. 22. "The White Belltrees No. 2". presented June 1, 1918 by Messrs. H. E. A. & V. White, "Belltrees", Scone. *C. A. Baker.*

taking of the desert bird's eggs.

Yours faithfully,
H. L. White."[25]

Despite the grim position there was always room in "H. L.'s" thoughts for his beloved egg collection.

It was by no means an easy time to relinquish any labour from "Belltrees". Labour was already scarce because of the War and the strike and on top of this, it was the worst season since 1888, but, nonetheless, "the firm" continued to help the War effort. The women on "Belltrees" were all busy knitting and they held Red Cross jumble sales and fetes on the homestead lawn. In August, 1916, H. E. A. & V. White were amongst the first to give a battle plane to Britain for the use of our men in France. A year later, "H. L." appealed to his brother Victor,

> ". . . if we were able to do anything in the actual fighting line, I'd not press the point . . . but as we can assist only in donations, I think it is up to us to give all we can possibly spare . . ."[26]

The following year, the partnership donated a second battle plane to Britain. Through "H. L.'s" letters during this period there is generally a worrying tone. It was difficult to manage large tracts of land with one's best employees away in the War, the prospect of Closer Settlement ever looming and the dread of crippling taxes hanging overhead. I shall say more later about "H. L.'s" famous stamp and bird skin collections; but it was at this time in 1917, that he decided to donate both of them to the nation. The precious bird skin collection, comprising over 5,000 skins worth many thousands of pounds, was carefully packed in five special cabinets and left the billiard room at "Belltrees", taken by a horse-drawn waggon to the Scone Railway Station on July 26, 1917, and railed to Melbourne. The cabinets were accompanied by the Curator, S. W. Jackson, who helped unpack the collection at the National Museum in Melbourne. Similarly, earlier in the year, the famous H. L. White Australian Stamp Collection, then valued at £15,000, left "Belltrees" and was donated to the Mitchell Library in Sydney.

H. L. White now felt more relieved, sad that his collections refused.

When the War ended in 1918, there was a huge Peace Day celebration sports day held on the sports field at "Belltrees". Men who enlisted from "Belltrees" during the 1914–18 World War are forever remembered by the Roll of Honour in our "Belltrees" Chapel which reads:

ROLL OF HONOUR
St. James Church, Belltrees

World War I

S. Russell	W. C. Eipper	R. Greer
L. Cronin	A. Schmierer	J. Pirie
*J. Adams	H. Mitchell	W. H. Pinkerton
E. Kiley	F. Cobb	H. Cobb
J. A. Taylor	T. Quinn	W. H. McPhee
R. Wakeling	S. Mitchell	D. Quinn
D. Grant	Rev. Keith Norman	A. Cobb
C. Schmierer	G. Eipper	George Cobb
Max Cogg	Harold Tilse	Roy Tilse
Frank Mehan	James Meehan	Thomas Meehan

*Killed at Beaumetz, France 29.3.1917

This list is more than a reminder of those who served; it is a proud record of a small community in action. It is a reflection of the capacity of all Australians at that time to respond without regret.

Right: Mr. Frank Coffa in the National Museum of Victoria photographing specimens from the H. L. White bird skin Collection.

Above: Gregory McAlister Mathews by B. Gotto. 1929. Oil on canvas. *Courtesy of National Library of Australia.*

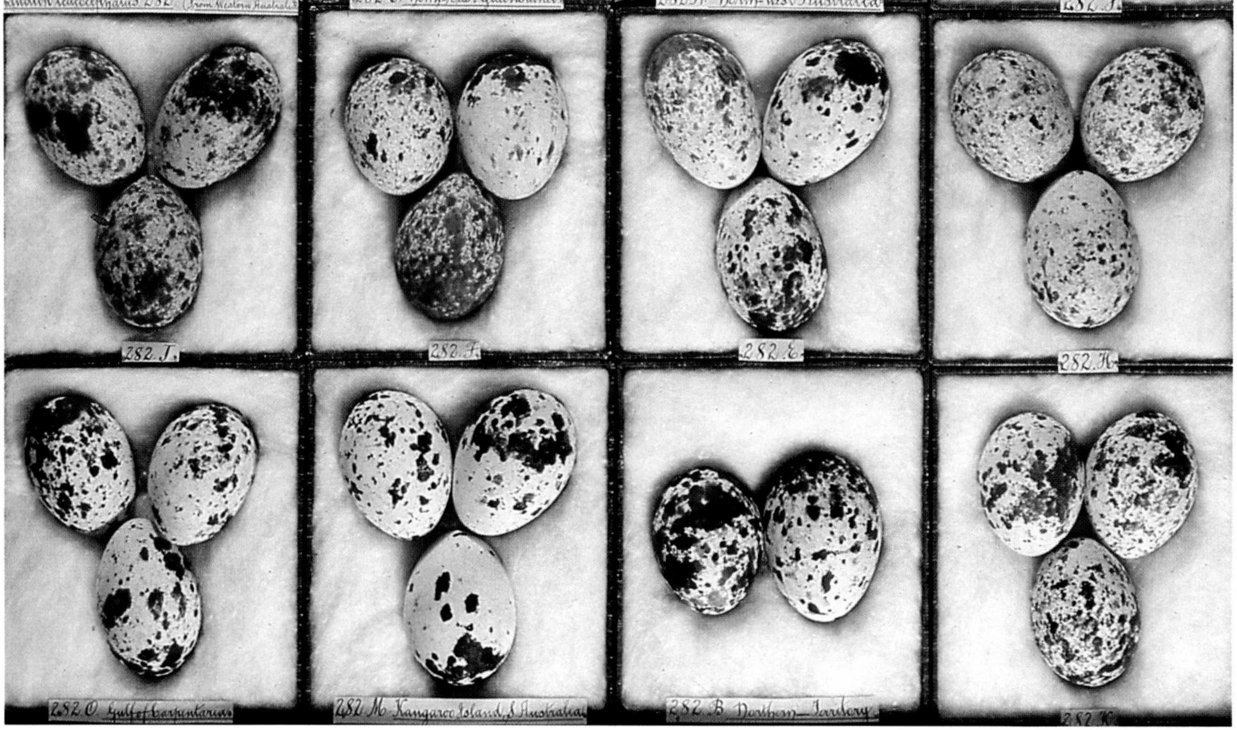

Drawer of Osprey eggs from the H. L. White bird egg Collection.
National Museum of Victoria. *Frank Coffa.*

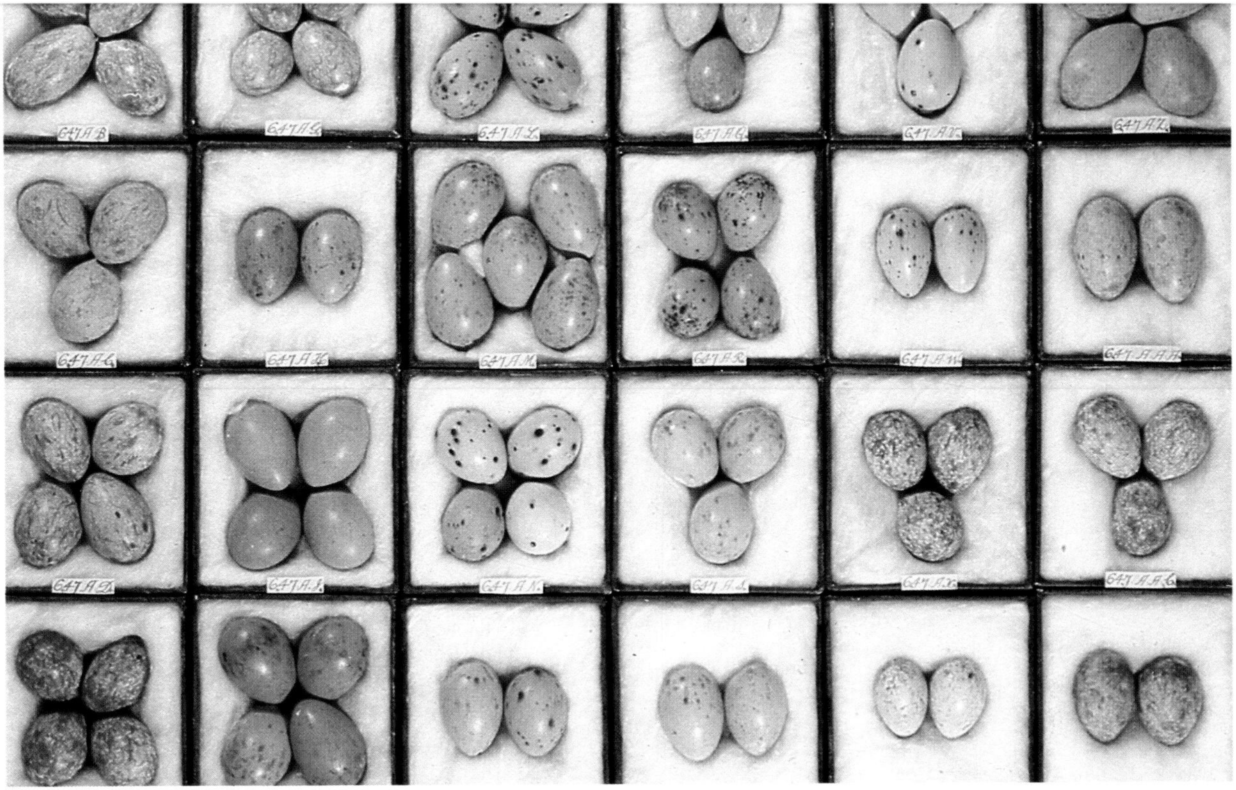

Drawer of Magpies' eggs from the H. L. White bird egg Collection. *Frank Coffa*.

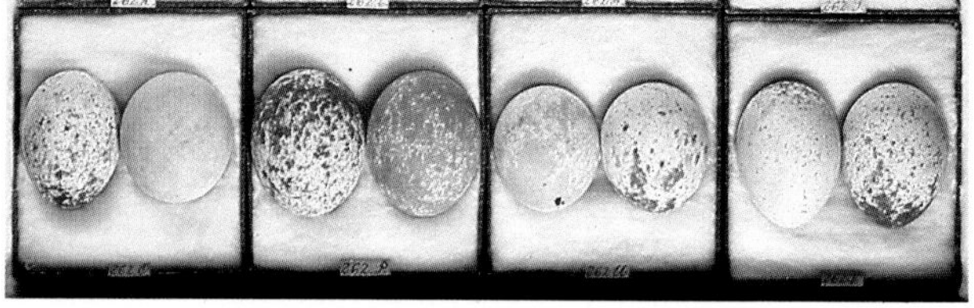

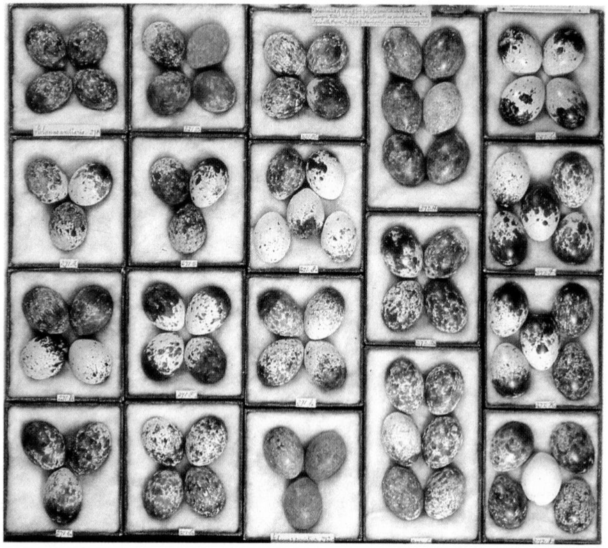

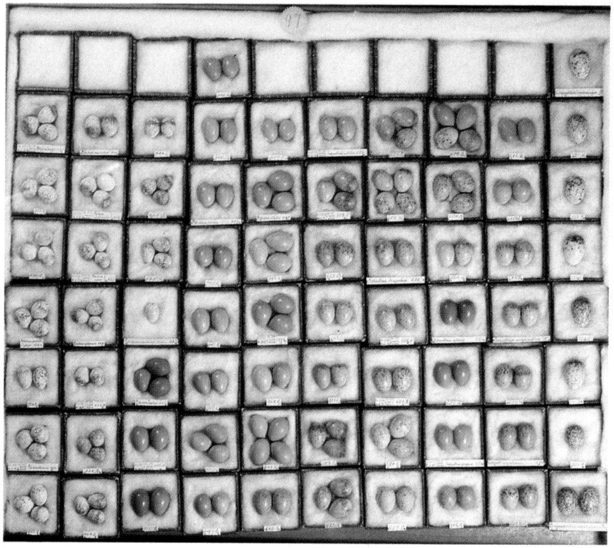

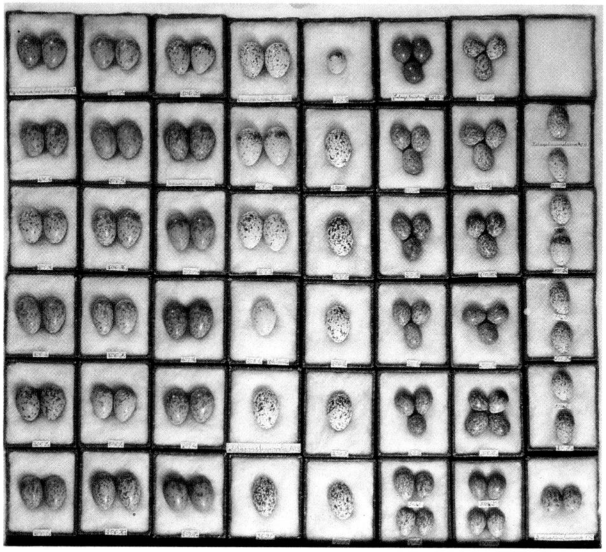

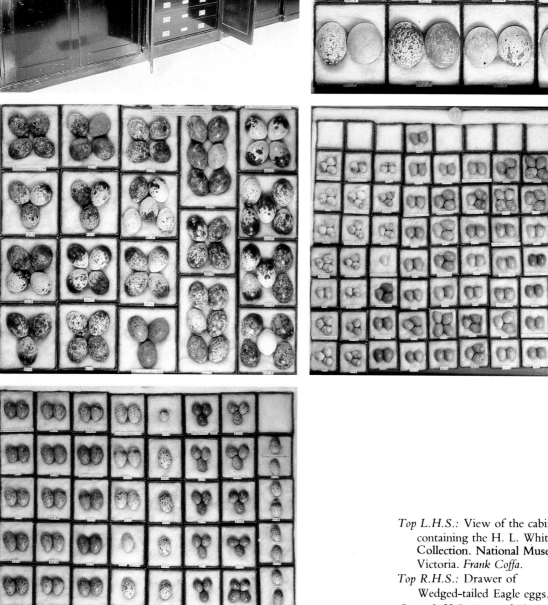

Top L.H.S.: View of the cabinets containing the H. L. White bird skin Collection. National Museum of Victoria. *Frank Coffa.*

Top R.H.S.: Drawer of Wedged-tailed Eagle eggs. *Frank Coffa.*

Centre L.H.S.: Eggs of Black Shouldered and Letter Wing Kites.

Centre R.H.S.: Robins eggs.

Bottom L.H.S.: Eggs of Cuckoo Shrikes (Caterpillar eaters).

TO THIS POINT, the dominant image of "Belltrees" is of a prosperous and expanding rural enterprise built by the application and initiative of many from an unfenced grant into a modern growing community. But there are many people for whom "Belltrees" has become synonymous with some of the greatest scientific collections ever assembled in Australia — H. L. White's collections of birds' eggs, bird skins and stamps. To these people, "Belltrees" is the place where these collections were put together.

It is not difficult to isolate the source of the overwhelming preoccupation that "H. L." developed for his collections. It was at Mr. Harborne Belcher's private school in Goulburn, the Garroorigang Grammar School, between the years of 1875 and 1878 that H. L. White was to develop interests which grew into life-long commitments. These interests were many and varied. In the first place Mr. Belcher was a fine cricketer having played for his County, Gloucestershire in England and it was he who pioneered the laying of the first turf wickets in Goulburn. Cricket was a must for the boys of "Garroorigang" and a love of cricket stayed with "H. L." throughout his life. As an adult, he attended every Test Match in Sydney for over twenty-five years and always sat in the same seat in the second row of the Members' Stand. He laid down a wicket at "Belltrees" and encouraged his only son "A. H." who later represented Cambridge University and New South Wales. When the opportunity presented itself, "H. L." could not resist the purchase in 1905 of a valuable collection of cricket books from F. M. Harpur of Cremorne.

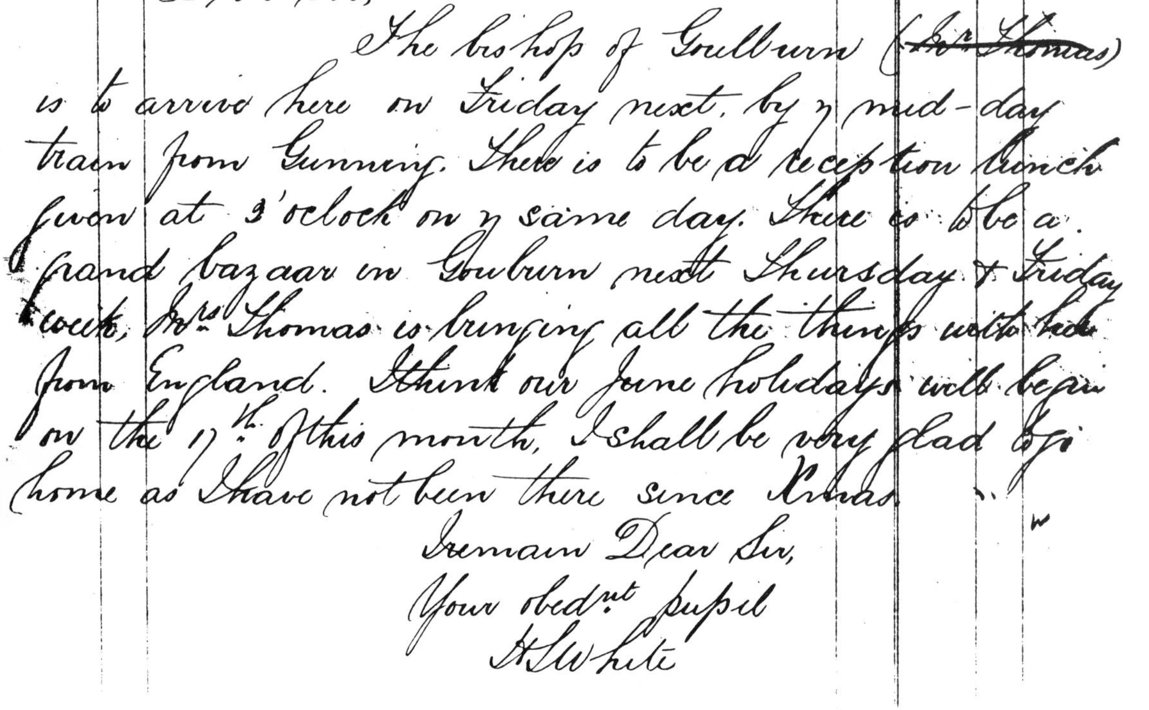
To S. H. Belcher Esqre

Dear Sir,

The bishop of Goulburn (~~Dr Thomas~~) is to arrive here on Friday next, by ye mid-day train from Gunning. There is to be a reception lunch given at 3 o'clock on ye same day. There is to be a grand bazaar in Goulburn next Thursday & Friday week, Mrs Thomas is bringing all the things with her from England. I think our June holidays will begin on the 17th of this month, I shall be very glad to go home as I have not been there since Xmas.

I remain Dear Sir,
Your obedt pupil
H L White

Page from H. L. White's school book. *Belltrees Library*.

All the boys at "Garroorigang" were required to write letters meticulously and regularly and this was a practice "H. L." carried through into his administration of "Belltrees". As someone who sought the history of "Belltrees" through fifty-four volumes of "H. L.'s" letters and accounts compiled over more than forty years, I can testify to the strength with which Mr. Belcher must have pressed his belief in the virtues of letter writing.

Almost as an extension of this emphasis on letter writing, Mr. Belcher taught his boys the importance of occupying their time in the pursuit of hobbies. It was he who first introduced "H. L." to collecting stamps and birds' eggs. In 1875 "H. L.", as a school boy, put together his first birds' egg collection which remains today in a special cabinet in the homestead. "H. L." so valued this first introduction to his interest in ornithology that he requested, in a special paragraph of his Will, that this boyhood collection should always remain at "Belltrees". Little did Mr. Belcher realise then that these boyhood interests would one day blossom into great national collections.

Mr. Harborne Belcher, Headmaster, Garroorigang School, Goulburn. *Kindly lent by Mr. Stuart Hume.*

The career of H. L. White did not admit to simple explanations. He lost his father in his first year at "Garroorigang" and soon learned the virtue and necessity of standing on one's own feet. He had an inquiring mind especially on scientific matters. He was always wanting to know why and was never satisfied until the answer contained its own proof. In later life he drove museum staff mad demanding identification of native species of grasses, trees, insects and birds. It was undoubtedly his recognition of the importance of his own education in his formative years which led "H. L." to be so supportive of education in the Upper Hunter. Whenever he got the chance, he encouraged school children to become interested in natural science and set up a museum of natural sciences at the "Belltrees" school. He also did much for the public schools at "Ellerston", Woolooma and Stewart's Brook and bought 17 acres on the Scone/Gundy Road as a site for a high school. On November 6, 1964, the Scone High School was completed, and taken to the billiard room and shown the birds' egg collection.

The background to this egg collection is most satisfactorily explained in a letter written by "H. L." in 1911 to an enquirer.

> ". . . I started collecting about 1875, when a boy at school; and during a residence of three years near Goulburn, N.S.W., put together rather a good lot, but all end blown. I still have the school boy collection, carefully preserved in a special case. After leaving school, business prevented my doing anything much until I came to live at Belltrees in 1885, when I started to collect in a more thorough manner. In 1906, I purchased Mr. S. W. Jackson's collection, and a few years later Mr. D. Le Souef's fine lot also became my property. During the last four years, I have had men working for me in all parts of Australia and they have been the means of securing several birds and many eggs hitherto undescribed. My oological collection now consists of 788 species of Australian birds' eggs . . ."[1]

In the same letter, "H. L." made explicit to the Sydney Museum his feelings which were later to lead to his bird skin and egg collection going to the National Museum in Melbourne.

> ". . . I intend eventually, after I reach the 800 mark, to present the whole collection to some Australian museum, certainly not to Sydney while the present management is in office. Some of the leading officials are the most narrow minded, jealous individuals it is possible to find. Fancy, they've absolutely refused to give me any further help in identifying species; this is private of course . . .[2]

In 1907, H. L. White purchased the egg collection of S. W. Jackson and at the same time persuaded Jackson to become not only his curator but also his "Man Friday".

While the impetus for his egg collection derived initially from his days at "Garroorigang", it owed much to his acquisition of the S. W. Jackson collection and from both of these evolved his interest in the collection of bird skins. Collectors were sent out by "H. L." either for eggs or skins. One of "H. L.'s" many letters concerning

The Belltrees public school, 1901. The children come from the property or adjoining lands. There are 31 pupils at the Belltrees school today.

between that of an actor and an Italian count. He is not a bushman in the ordinary sense of the word but knows his way about and is the only man who has found eggs of an Eastern Atrichia. In fact he is the best scrub collector I know . . ."[4]

S. W. Jackson was a brilliant natural scientist. He was a large man of 16½ stone and it was amazing how he had such success climbing trees and moving through the undergrowth, tracking down minute scrub birds. "H. L." nicknamed his friend "the Professor" or "Pro" and referred to him as such to fellow ornithologists when writing accounts of the progress of his collections. "Pro" was not without a lighter and a melancholy side to his nature. He was an amusing, light hearted fellow, often allowing himself to be the buffoon in order to entertain "the boss" with mimicry of bird calls and ventriloquial tricks that relaxed "H. L." and enabled him to unwind. But he was also a fearful hypochondriac when he mourned his ill health and dwelt upon his woes. On these occasions, "H. L." would become very impatient and irritable.

". . . Pro is laid up, with imaginitis I think, got a chill, in bed, no loss of appetite; no pain, found him in bed, looked like a big buck seal, rolled up in a blanket, doors and windows wide open, room clean, fresh and tidy. After talking for a time, he asked me what I thought of his pictures, a nice array of pretty bird illustrations, etc. I then took a glance at his dressing table where stood a large photo frame quite alone in front of the glass — of the dear old boy himself. That was about the extreme limit, so I left without saying another word, but felt like emptying the water jug over him . . ."[5]

Nonetheless, as part of the community of "single fellows" within "Belltrees", "Pro" was often the life of the party. Indeed, "H. L." was so impressed with the concerts that they organised, that he gave timber and building materials and in 1921 the "single fellows" built the entertainment hall. This was much in use on Saturday nights, a meeting place for miles around. Many stories are still told today of practical jokes that breathed humour and

"Professor" S. W. Jackson giving Mrs. H. L. White a lesson in Oology. 1924.
H. L. White

It is part of the "Belltrees" ethic that the boss works alongside his employees. So it was with "H. L.", Ernest, Arthur and Victor. They were all adept at branding, dehorning, mustering, classing and fencing. As I have said, there were many single men working for them and, for amusement, they enjoyed playing practical jokes on their fellow workers. Often, "the bosses" were not immune.

One day, the men filled an empty post hole with water, sprinkled dry sheep manure thickly on the surface, and watched "H. L." walk right into it. Another day, out mustering, Mr. "A. G." saw an idle stockman in the distance, sitting on his horse, doing nothing. He repeatedly called to him, no answer. In anger, he rode up close to find a dead horse propped up and a human dummy in the saddle. The same human dummy was used on another occasion. This time it hung from a rope on the limb of a tree visible from the Stewart's Brook road. Being the local Magistrate, "H. L." was called to the scene late at night. He was not amused. More often than not, Victor, the youngest brother, encouraged the men in their pranks, and bet one of the employees at "Ellerston" £5 that he would not dare christen his new son "Henry Ernest Arthur Victor". The man did and Henry Ernest Arthur Victor Taylor is alive to this day.

But for S. W. Jackson, the ornithological task was ever present. He enjoyed being released from the arduous cataloguing necessary at "Belltrees" to return to his field work collecting eggs or bird skins in many States. When the curator was away on these expeditions, "H. L." would wait eagerly at the office for the daily mail coach to arrive, hoping there would be letters and packages from S. W. Jackson or his other collectors all over Australia.

In 1919, "H. L." sent "S. W. J." to Beaudesert in Queensland to hunt down the Eastern Atrichia. Seven years earlier, he had sent Jackson to Albany in Western Australia looking for the rest of the Atrichia Clamosa or Western Rufous Scrub Bird. "The Pro" had been unsuccessful in the hunt and assumed that the small bird had been wiped out by wild cats and bush fires. Remembering this incident, and not hearing any positive results from "S. W. J." in evidence of this discovery was the fact that both the huge naturalist and the tiny Atrichonis were ventriloquists. The bird had eluded hunters by imitating their whistles, and throwing his own call from the scrub to the tree tops. When eventually "S. W. J." tracked the female down, he wrote jubilantly in his notebook that evening:

> "It was after four weeks of constant and most diligent searching. We visited our most favourite locality early on the morning of the 17th and could find no sign of the male bird. He was silent and possibly feeding with the female. But experience would lead to the assumption that when he called he was not with or near the female and when he remained silent for hours or days then he was most of his time with her, thus giving no clue as to where she was. At 3.30 p.m., he started his shrill notes again in the gully where we had often seen him. We sat on the ground and listened for a few moments. He was under the rubbish only some forty feet west of us. Suddenly, he became silent and in a short time started to call again some forty yards to the east. This appeared to me very curious and unusual. I concluded he had met the female when he moved from where we first heard him calling . . . when all at once we heard a faint sound and saw another Atrichonis. At this moment, the male was calling loudly nearly 100 feet away . . . After twenty minutes of careful watching and intense anxiety, I fired from a distance of about 15 feet and the bird fell, beautifully shot, not a mark on her, and not a feather or drop of blood lost."[7]

After this victory, "S. W. J." obeyed orders and moved camp. But, unfortunately, on his return trip to Brisbane he received a bad kick in the stomach from a pack horse and this necessitated "the Pro" to undergo an operation. This time his melancholia was genuine.

In a more amplified commentary on "H. L.'s" ornithological collection which appears as an appendix to this book, A. R. McEvey, Curator of Birds at the National Museum in Victoria says:

> ". . . The H. L. White Egg Collection contains over 4,200 clutches of eggs of Australian birds housed in a beautifully

Jack Ramsay and J. Bettington (Jnr.) returning from a day's collecting at Wallis Lake.
Kindly lent by Jack Ramsay.

Collecting the eggs of the White-bellied sea-eagle, using S. W. Jackson's rope ladder.

paper more suitable words to express
to you my deep appreciation for your
exceedingly kind & thoughtful gift to me
in the form of the Cabinet that at one time
contained the "Jacksonian Oological Collection",
and purchased by you in 1907.
I was too overcome with surprise & delight
to say much this morning when you so
kindly made the gift to me, so please
do not think I was not most deeply
grateful because I did not say much
in reply. I could only think at the
time of your goodness to me, & I consequently
said very little. I am happy to have this
Cabinet again, & it will always bring back
to me most happy recollections of your
family, your home at Belltrees, and
your very good self. Yours very truly
Sid. Wm. Jackson

This letter found in the cabinet of "Jacksonian Oological Collection"
at the Arthur Rylah Institute Melbourne.
Courtesy The Arthur Rylah Institute.

H. J. Campbell, expressing both the concerns and the complications associated with getting rid of his bird skin collection. It was war time and "H. L." was looking to reducing his administrative burdens at "Belltrees". The letter gives yet another insight into the different personalities of "H. L." and "the professor":

> ". . . I feel very sad at parting with my friends, the skins, and have been talked to more than a little about sending them out of my native State; my sole idea however is to place the collection where it may readily be referred to by members of the R.A.O.U. Further, I hope to add materially to it from time to time. I laid the foundations of the collection by the purchase of Mr. Lancelot Harrison's specimens, later on adding those of Messrs. Blakelly and Robert Grant, the collection of the latter containing many rare species, and everything splendidly prepared. Many well known collectors such as Captain S. A. White, Messrs. H. G. Barnard, F. L. Whitlock, L. G. Chandler, G. F. Hill and W. McLennan have added materially to my numbers. If you require any other particulars, why not ask S. W. J. when he visits your city next week. Jackson loves publicity and attention. I hate both. If the R.A.O.U. thinks it owes me any little civility, S. W. J. will be on hand to receive it. The Union will never get hold of me, so it had better take Sidney William as a substitute . . ."[9]

"H. L." was indeed conscious of the debt he owed Jackson for he had become an institution at "Belltrees", not only for his cataloguing of the collections and his ability to break through the stoic facade of "H. L."; but also for the many items around the homestead today which have been accurately documented by "the professor". However, in reflecting on the devotion shared by "H. L." and "the professor" in putting the collections together, my sympathy falls upon Mrs. "H. L." and the children, Dorothy, Norah and "A. H.". One cannot help feel that while Australia's ornithological horizons may have been widened, the childhood pleasures of "H. L.'s" children were reduced.

For in setting up a collection, a volume of correspondence alone is involved — letters to collectors in the field, to ornithologists, to curators and reports to friends. It was one such

Henry Charles White, with whom he had played as a child at "Belltrees". The packaging of the emu skin began a sequence of letters that lasted through two decades. G. M. Mathews, who was born in Dubbo, New South Wales, in 1876, and educated at The King's School, Parramatta, sailed for England with his wife and her two children from a previous marriage in 1902 for the Coronation of Edward VII. In England, he decided to emulate John Gould and produce a grand illustrated modern work on the birds of Australia. The ensuing thick twelve volumes became his life's work. "H. L." did much to help Mathews by lending him bird skin specimens; by backing his bona fides before the publication of his books in Australia, and by assisting him in his attempts to sell the Mathews Bird Skin Collection of 30,000 species together with his famous ornithological library when Mathews fell into bad economic times. "H. L." tried valiantly to keep these two collections within Australia and prevent them from being sold to America. What "H. L." did for Mathews, he argued, he did in the name of science, for the two men often fought outrageously and the correspondence between them bears witness to this. In December, 1912, "H. L." wrote to Mathews in part,

> ". . . in your present letter I am 'unsportsmanlike', 'quick to believe any cock and bull yarn', 'unwilling and unable to be just', 'speaking upon subjects I know nothing of', etc. etc. I note with pleasure that you omit arsony and forgery . . . again, how do you arrive at the decision that my collection of Regent birds' eggs has done more harm than Bell's shooting? My 33 sets took twenty-five years to collect and are from a stretch of country at least five hundred miles long and twenty miles wide that is, six and a half millon acres. Your birds are taken within a few months from a small island of some 9,000 acres . . ."[10]

It was well known that "G. M. M." was a tactless, dictatorial sort of man and, as "H. L." said himself, thought himself the "I am" of Australian ornithology. But the constant haranguing from one to the other only tended to sharpen the talons and talents of

wrote to the Secretary of the Australian Museum in Sydney in 1912.

> "Sir,
> Kindly inform me whether I am still under the boycott as imposed by your Curator in his letter of 30th March, 1911. The farce has been continued quite long enough and if I am still refused information by a public institution, such as yours is, I shall appeal to the government for an explanation . . ."[11]

Which he did, and it was because of North and his narrow minded views that "H. L." determined to donate his collections to Melbourne.

> ". . . I intend to present the whole collection to some Australian museum but certainly not to Sydney while the present management is in office. . . ."[12]

It hurt "H. L." bitterly to send his oological and bird skin collections outside his own State.

> ". . . but if the official in charge is not obliging, one gets very little encouragement or help. Anyway, such is my unfortunate experience with the Sydney Museum. The consequence is, that that institution has lost all chance of securing about £10,000 worth (in current values $330,000) of stuff from me."[13]

Sadly for posterity, this hurt ran far more deeply within "H. L." than was realised. It caused him to write into the conditions of the gift of the bird skin collection to Melbourne that "no specimen is permitted to leave this museum". "H. L." feared constant usage from Sydney.

Often Mathews was the victim of "H. L.'s" wrath, more often than not generated as a result of competition between the two men. On one occasion, "H. L." got so angry with "G. M. M." that he refused to allow him into his house. But the resentment did

Three famous Ornithologists in the Belltrees garden. 22nd May, 1921 – A. J. Campbell, H. L. White and N. W. Cayley. *Dorothy Minell.*

eggs must always be remembered. These are placed on the list as 'Whitei' etc., a fitting tribute to the owner. A book on the eggs of Australian birds can only be written with this collection near at hand, and all the world waits for such a book by Henry Luke White of Belltrees, the owner of this unique treasure. May such a book be done in the near future.

Gregory Macalister Mathews.
24.4.1914."[14]

G. M. Mathews held a high appreciation of the good things in life but sometimes they were enjoyed at other peoples' expense. He had a lovely home in England, filled with fine pieces of furniture; he hunted twice a week, and put together a brilliant ornithological collection of books from all over the world. But for financial reasons, by 1918, it became necessary for him to offer both his bird skin and book collection for sale. "H. L." wished fervently that this bird skin collection of 30,000 specimens be returned to Australia. "G. M. M." demanded £8,000. "H. L." wrote to Sir Baldwin Spencer at the Melbourne Museum but World War I was still in progress, taxes were high and extra finance was going into compulsory War Loans. In addition, many Australian ornithologists resented the price demanded by Mathews when they knew that many of the species had been collected through Australian Government permits. Eventually, the collection was not sold in Australia but was purchased by Lord Rothschild in England. "H. L." wrote to the Mitchell Library in Sydney and tried to persuade the Trustees to purchase Mathews' ornithological library, but without success. After the failure of these attempts, "G. M. M." became despondent about ever completing his series of "Birds of Australia". He was now up to volume seven, and "H. L." encouraged him to continue.

By 1925, Mathews was forced to sell his home "Foulis Court". "This will break my heart," he wrote to "H. L.", "and leave me a wanderer of the earth again, especially as it means that so many, if not all of my household goods must go. These of course can never be replaced." In 1932, Mathews learned to his dismay purpose of seeing the Mathews' Collection. A librarian escorted me to the lower levels, unlocked a caged door and there I stood transfixed amid this famous ornithological library. I wished at that moment that "H. L." had been beside me. He had wanted so much for these books to be in Australia and not America, and he would have been so proud of his friend's decision to overcome the temptation of monetary gain in order to perpetuate this magnificent collection in Australia. I looked along the shelves and saw the leather-bound volumes with "G. M. M." on their spine. Mathews had always demanded quality and perfection. I was particularly delighted to know that 890 photographic glass negatives on natural history subjects, mainly birds, taken by S. W. Jackson are incorporated in the pictorial material section of the Mathews' Collection. It is encouraging to know that "H. L." has made a small contribution to this ornithological treasure chest.

Within Australia today there is a great re-awakening in the interests of birds. As I hear ornithological discussions around me, I cannot help but think back to the numerous letters that travelled between "Foulis Court", Winchester, England, and "Belltrees", Scone, Australia, from 1908 to 1927. How lucky the ornithologist of today is to have the research and reference material that is available now through the efforts of H. L. White and G. M. Mathews.

Of the two H. L. White collections of birds' eggs and bird skins, A. R. McEvey, Curator of Birds at the National Museum in Victoria, has said,

> ". . . These two collections are national assets in ornithology and are not matched in their condition, coverage or data by privately formed collections in any other Australian institution . . . H. L. White was a true collector who valued both the use of his collections for the purpose of research and their presentation and preservation for their intrinsic significance and appeal as ornithological collections . . ."[15]

The bird skin collection was forwarded to the National Museum in Melbourne during World War I. But because the birds' egg collection was "H. L.'s" special love, it only left the billiard possessed more cheek." He preferred to remain in the confines of his office and library writing copious letters to friends and acquaintances. His home was functional and unadorned; he preferred corresponding with people rather than inviting them to stay or dine. On one occasion, H. L. White's best friend, J. H. Bettington of Merriwa, wrote and asked "H. L." to join him on a fishing trip. Bettington received the following reply,

> "14th March, 1920.
> To J. H. Bettington, Terragong, Merriwa.
>
> > . . . I am too unsociable and standoffish to fit in anywhere. Let me know please just what date suits you. Then, if you feel inclined to indulge my humour, I will try and fix up matters so as to get away for a short time. If I'm likely to be a square peg in a round hole, put me off at once. I will not be annoyed in the least."[17]

H. L. White found it difficult to relax in the company of others and felt he had to pay financially for any kindness or courtesy given to him. I often wonder if, deep down, "H. L." longed to be more outward going and capable of enjoying more the pleasure he gave. He avoided any public attention and when he gave his two Australian collections to the nation in 1917, he sent his curator, S. W. Jackson, to Melbourne with the bird skins and his solicitor, A. C. Ebsworth, to the Mitchell Library in Sydney to hand over the H. L. White New South Wales Stamp Collection. On both occasions, H. L. White sent his apologies for being absent.

A great part of H. L. White's life was spent in the pursuit of his hobbies and in acting out the role of scientist. He not only became fascinated by all the natural sciences but also he regarded philately as a science as well — the science of collecting postage stamps. He believed, like his friend E. Van Weenan that, ". . . (philately) teaches history, geography, numismatics, and the art of printing and colours; it instils in the mind powers of great observation, patience and correct method."[18] It is no surprise then that each

View from the balcony of the new homestead looking down the lawn to the original homestead. This is where Louisa Maude White sat whilst convalescing. *Laurence Le Guay.*

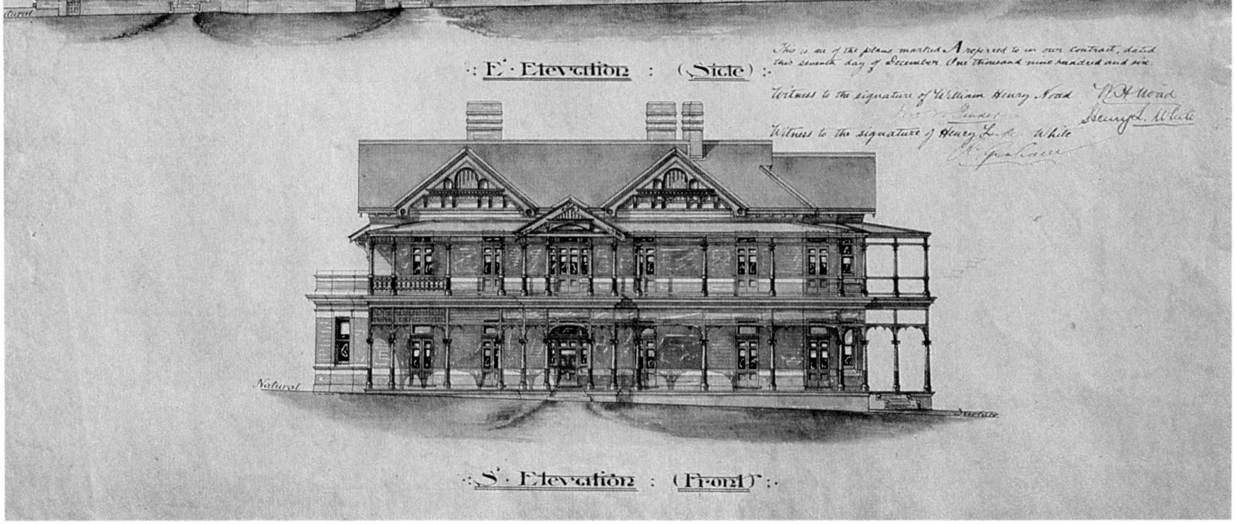

Final plan of Belltrees homestead by architect J. W. Pender. 1906.
Kindly lent from the files of Ian Pender.

Plan number two submitted to H. L. White by J. W. Pender 1905.
Kindly lent from the files of Ian Pender.

The new homestead marries with the old buildings; a green lawn unites them. *Laurence Le Guay*.

The "Belltrees" homestead nestles comfortably into the undulating hills of the Upper Hunter Ranges. *Laurence Le Guay.*

know all about the methods of printing, perforation, shade varieties, marginal markings, the position of errors etc. . . . which cannot be studied thoroughly except in sheets or large blocks. Almost every issue of *The London Philatelist* brings under notice the advisability of studying stamps in sheets . . ."[19]

H. L. White enjoyed it all, but in 1917, he was deeply concerned about World War I and considered selling his stamp collection in England in order to give the proceeds to the War Fund. He was advised that the collection, as such, would suffer; that the value he would receive would be two-thirds of its intrinsic worth and if necessary would be split up. That is when "H. L." decided to give his beloved New South Wales Postal and Fiscal Stamp Collection to his home State of New South Wales. He offered it to the Trustees of the Mitchell Library, and the offer was received. "H. L." handed over his priceless albums. Discussions then proceeded as to the way in which the stamp collection should be presented. "H. L." offered to donate cabinets of Australian wood in order to house the stamps and upon the advice of the philatelist Mr. Fred Hagen, a Mr. Jones of Messrs. Jones and Pike made the cabinets. Four of them were made out of Queensland Maple, containing 44 horizontal slides, each slide capable of holding four sheets of stamps — 176 frames in all. When completed, Mr. Wright, the Mitchell Librarian, positioned the cabinets in the centre of the room, back to back, so as to maximise the light and receive no shadows. By January, 1918, the Trustees wanted a public function to hand over the completed H. L. White Postal Stamp Collection. The Librarian informed the donor, "H. L.", of their intentions. H. L. White's reply was predictable if surprising:

> ". . . I do not wish to take any part in the official handing over of the H. L. White Philatelic Collection. I'd far rather give you another collection than face the ordeal of a public function. The thing is quite out of my line. If someone is required to represent me, my solicitor will have to do it."[20]

The handing over duly went ahead in the presence of the

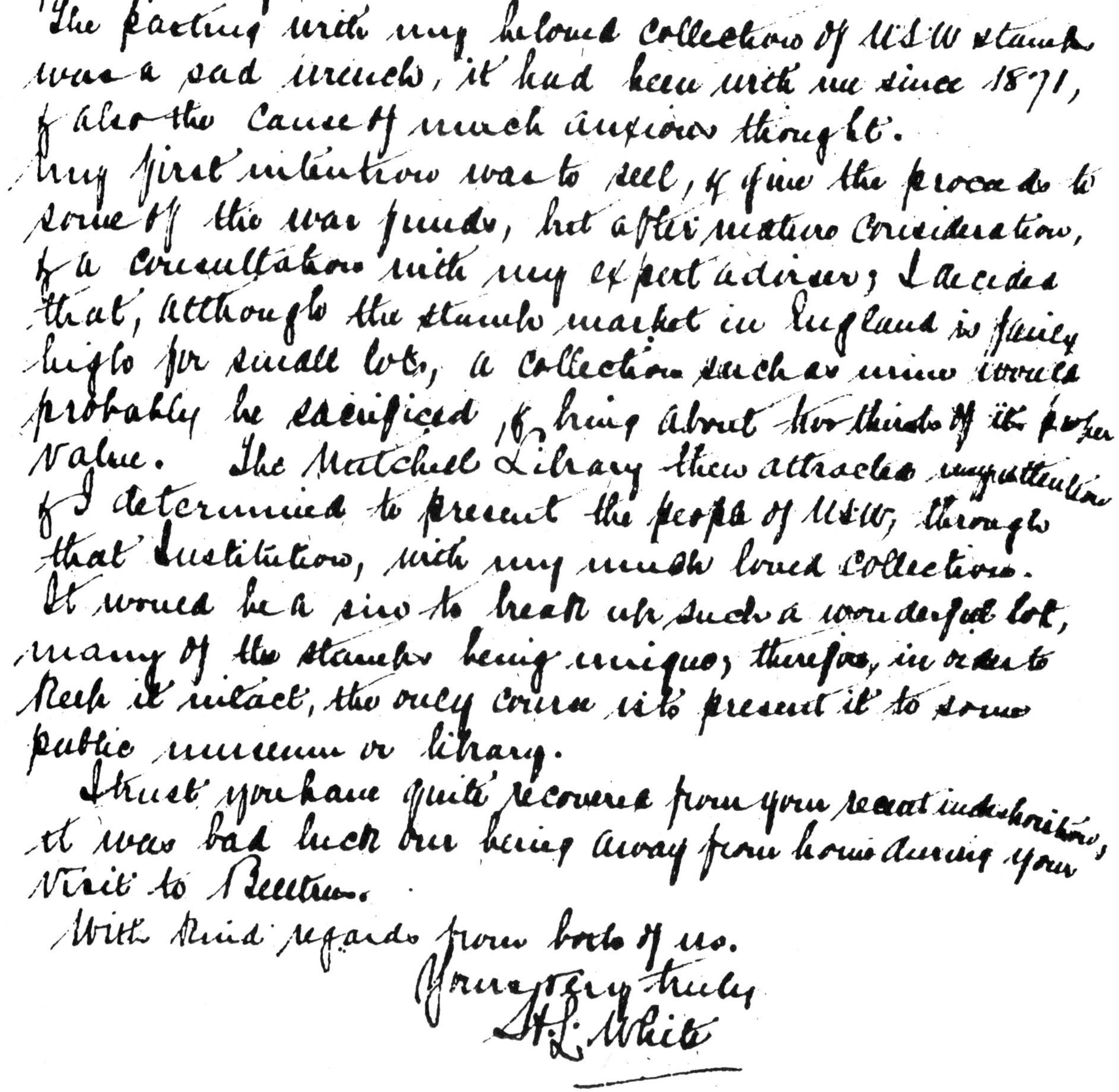

The parting with my beloved Collection of N.S.W. stamps was a sad wrench, it had been with me since 1871, & also the cause of much anxious thought.

My first intention was to sell, & give the proceeds to some of the War funds, but after mature consideration, & a consultation with my expert advisers, I decided that, although the stamp market in England is fairly high for small lots, a Collection such as mine would probably be sacrificed, & bring about two thirds of its proper value. The Mitchell Library then attracted my attention & I determined to present the people of N.S.W., through that Institution, with my much loved Collection.

It would be a sin to break up such a wonderful lot, many of the stamps being unique; therefore, in order to keep it intact, the only course is to present it to some public museum or library.

I trust you have quite recovered from your recent indisposition, it was bad luck our being away from home during your visit to Belltrees.

With kind regards from both of us.

Yours very truly

H. L. White

One of the 54,000 letters written by H. L. White. There is an altar chair in the Belltrees chapel in memory of Dr. Stretch, Bishop of Newcastle.

important donations to its public collections . . . not only would the large and ever increasing body of philatelists of Australia be delighted with such a collection as the world renowned H. L. White Collection . . . but the citizens of the State generally would appreciate the gift and the self denial of the collector which inspired it . . . it was characteristic of great collectors like Mr. White . . . that they should desire to avoid notoriety and public demonstrations. It was indeed not easy to persuade Mr. White to approve the public opening of his collection and it was altogether characteristic that his excessive modesty prompted him not to take a personal part in that ceremony. Together with the gift of the stamps themselves, Mr. White had undertaken to defray the whole cost of furniture for the exhibition. This amounted to no inconsiderable sum. Mr. White allowed the Principal Librarian to decide on the methods of displaying and safeguarding the collection suggesting only that he should confer with his old friend and philatelic adviser, Mr. F. Hagen, and expressing the desire that the cabinets should be made of Australian timber . . . they felt deeply indebted to Mr. White for his patriotic and generous gift . . ."[21]

The Lieutenant-Governor, in conclusion, commented that,

". . . the place where we stand is the work of a devoted, patriotic Australian, who presented to Australia one of the most interesting collections imagineable . . ."[22]

When I visited the Mitchell Library to read the whole text of Mr. Arthur Dowling's address that he delivered on behalf of the Trustees at the ceremony, I felt saddened. I held in my hands the exact small pages from which the President had read and I resented, in a way, that "H. L.'s" excessive modesty had prevented him from being present on that day. He had sent A. C. Ebsworth to deputise for him and he had insisted that his friend, Mr. Fred Hagen, be there too and that he should wear a frock coat and tall hat. "H. L." wanted Hagen's devoted assistants, the Misses Pines, Nellie and Elsie, to be there too, for they had helped "H. L." purchase stamps for his New South Wales Collection. "H. L." was so anxious to know how it all went that he made each friend

"H. L." had purchased the well known "Inverted Swan" West Australian stamp for £450 and regarded it as a good investment. He was right. Today, this stamp realises over $120,000.[23] A stamp of the same printing (W.A., 4^{d}, 1854, Blue.) with "Australia" squeezed into half its height is also in the Collection and is valued today at $80,000.[24] By this time, "H. L." had given his Tasmanian Stamp Collection to his daughter Norah, Mrs. H. V. Hordern. But in July, 1922, he persuaded her to donate this to the nation for incorporation in the H. L. White Stamp Collection. Norah consented. It was a most noble gesture on her part for she was separated from her husband, bringing up two sons and the collection she gave at that time to the Mitchell Library was valued at £2,000. When "H. L." had disposed of all his Australian Collection, he wrote to Mr. Wright, the Librarian of the Mitchell Library, in January, 1923:

> "Please accept my best thanks for all the trouble and interest you have taken in the matter of my stamps. You, however, now have the satisfaction of knowing that the Mitchell Library possesses a collection of New South Wales, Queensland, West Australian and Tasmanian postage stamps equal to anything in the world. I got into a certain amount of hot water with the family for giving such a valuable collection away but I am satisfied that I did the right thing in presenting it to the nation. All private collections must be broken up sooner or later whereas the H. L. White lot will remain intact forever."[25]

In the same year, the members of the Philatelic Club in Sydney had an evening at the Mitchell Library to view the now National Collection. This time, H. L. White chose to attend and Mr. Bassett-Hull gave an address on the history of stamps. He highlighted the early issues of the Collection:

> "Their crude execution and the retouches on the plates are of the greatest interest . . ."[26]

Mr. Bassett-Hull also praised Mr. H. L. White's patriotism not only as revealed in the donation of his stamp collection, but also

Ceremony of the presentation of the H. L. White Postage Stamp Collection at Mitchell Library. 23.1.1918.

as evidenced in his Australian bird collection and his extensive library of rare Australian books.

"H. L." continued his interest in philately, collecting stamps of the Irish Free State, the Australian Commonwealth and the North-West Pacific. His name was placed on the Roll of Distinguished World Philatelists and by 1925, the H. L. White Stamp Collection of the Australian Commonwealth had risen in value to £50,000. Mr. Paul Brunton of the Manuscript Department of the Mitchell Library in Sydney wrote only last year about the Collection:

> "The H. L. White Postage Stamp Collection is housed in Mitchell Library, the Department of the State Library of New South Wales which specialises in the collection of materials relating to Australia and the Pacific . . . it can be viewed by any member of the public providing a written application is made and appropriate identification is produced. A member of staff remains in attendance while the collection is being examined. These measures are necessary due to the great value and rarity of many of the items . . . it has been insured for $2 million . . . the collection has been used by those researching for television programmes, newspaper articles and more scholarly works on philately."[27]

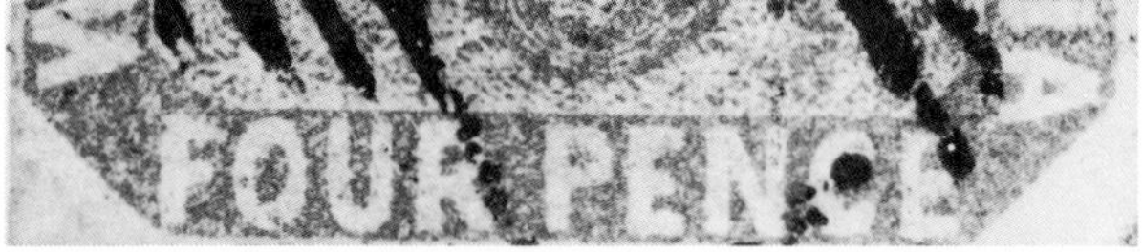

H. L. White's efforts were widely recognised in his day but to the end he remained unwilling to be elevated in public esteem explaining that,

> "I do not consider it right that just because a man happens to be a trifle better off than the average, he should receive applause for spending a little of what he has on others. Why should I receive any thanks and be made appear better than I really am."[28]

In a sense he was right. For the products of his labours live on after him, inscribing indelibly the name of H. L. White into Australia's recorded history.

Three valuable postage stamps – "The Inverted Swan" W.A., The W.A. 1854 Blue, and "Queen Victoria Blackeye". *Courtesy Mitchell Library.*

"Belltrees" Homestead

THERE IS NO DOUBT that the compilation of the collections dominated life within the "Belltrees" homestead. The anxiety of cataloguing correctly each bird skin, bird's egg or stamp obviously permeated the atmosphere of "H. L.'s" home. And besides all that, there was the onerous task of managing a large 220,000 acre property.

The variety and particularity of "H. L.'s" interests can do nothing but evoke a profound sense of admiration for the patience of his wife. Imagine how many hours she must have spent listening to anecdotes being told at meal times by S. W. Jackson, the curator, and "H. L."; or being invited to marvel at a new egg or bird skin recently arrived at the "Belltrees" billiard room from a collector in a distant part of Australia. In 1887, H. L. White had married Louisa Maude Ebsworth, daughter of Edward Stanley Ebsworth of "Bronte House", Waverley, Sydney. Earlier, in 1882, James Cobb White of "Edinglassie", "H. L.'s" brother, had married the eldest Ebsworth daughter, Emmeline Eliza; and in 1893, "H. L.'s" younger brother, Arthur, married Millicent Ebsworth — in all, three Ebsworth sisters married to three White brothers.

But the connection between the Ebsworth and White families was not just a marital one. As far back as the 1820s, the grandfathers on both sides had been pioneers together in the "A. A." Company grant at Stroud. In the 1850s, James Ebsworth became a wool broker and there still exists in the "Belltrees" library today hand-written wool liens recording the sale of the manded the troop of "Belltrees" employees on "Belltrees"-bred horses. He was killed in action fighting for the Commonwealth in 1900 and a band of loyal supporters clubbed together and financed the erection of a memorial at "Belltrees" Chapel in his honour. There is also a memorial to him in The King's School Chapel at Parramatta. It is little wonder that when, in 1901, a son was born to Mrs. H. L. White he was named Alfred Henry Ebsworth White after his heroic uncle.

Another younger Ebsworth was Norman Ebsworth. He was a massive fellow and a great cricketer. He played for New South Wales and was well remembered as a powerful batsman. While he was a stock and station agent in Scone, Norman Ebsworth auctioned cattle and land for H. E. A. & V. White. In fact, in 1913, when the Ebsworth's "Marooan" estate in Scone was subdivided, "H. L." named Joan Street, Scone, at the corner of the New England Highway and the Gundy Road, after Norman Ebsworth's only daughter. There are many connections between the two families but perhaps the member of the Ebsworth clan that "H. L." relied on most was A. C. (Charlie) Ebsworth, a cousin of the three sisters and a member of the firm of solicitors "Ebsworth and Ebsworth" in Sydney. There are volumes of letters addressed to "Dear Charlie". Just as the family doctor in the early part of the century had to be the family adviser, so did the family solicitor in the latter part of the century have to answer to many demands. I marvel that "Dear Charlie" had any time to devote to legal matters or briefs other than those numerous directives that came from "H. L." at "Belltrees". He dictated lengthy orders and wanted immediate attention. If the answers to his directives did not reach the G.P.O. at an appointed hour, and be in the "Belltrees" mailbag the next morning, A. C. Ebsworth would receive a blast.

When "H. L." refused to attend public functions, he sent Charles Ebsworth as his deputy; and, as I mentioned earlier, it was A. C. Ebsworth, not H. L. White, who officially handed over the H. L. White Stamp Collection to the Trustees of the

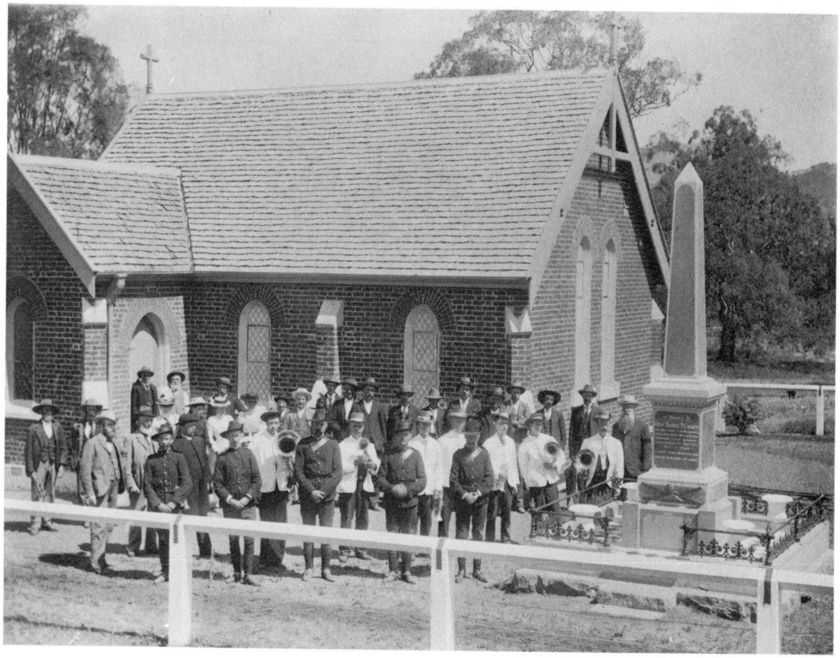

Above: Belltrees stockmen on Belltrees horses. Boer War, South Africa 1900. Station Brand [brand symbol] seen on shoulder of horse ridden by Lieutenant Alfred Ebsworth.

Right: Unveiling the Ebsworth monument at St. James' Church Belltrees. 4th November, 1901.

The business transactions of the White family became A. C. Ebsworth's particular obsession and he cherished his role. One day, when he was an elderly gentleman, he visited his firm "Ebsworth and Ebsworth" to be told that they were updating the office — the filing cabinets were to be streamlined. Purple with rage, the old man reportedly stormed from the room saying, "You can't do that. You can't put the Whites with the other Ws." Nothing could better exemplify than this my earlier remark that the association between the Whites and the Ebsworths extended far beyond that established through marriage.

When "H. L." and Mrs. White were first married, they lived in the original "Belltrees" homestead built by H. C. Sempill in 1836. It was in this building that their three children were born - two daughters, Dorothy Ebsworth White and Norah Ebsworth White; and in 1901, a son, Alfred Henry Ebsworth White. "H. L." was so excited at the birth of his heir that he decided to build a new homestead for his family. He wrote to the architect, J. W. Pender of Maitland on November 20, 1905:

> "Dear Sir,
> We have decided to erect a new residence here close to the old house and shall be glad to employ you if you can supply the plans etc. to our satisfaction and provided also that you lose no time about it . . . everything is to be good but plain. The whole brick building must be made to look well, nothing of the barn appearance about it . . . acetylene gas to be used throughout if practicable . . . electric bells where necessary . . . now hurry up and see what you can do for us.
>
> Yours faithfully,
> H. L. White."[4]

Ernest and Victor were still bachelors, and they too were to live in the new house; whereas Arthur was married and had built, in the 1890s, a brick home half a mile away which he called "Kioto" following a trip to Japan.

Above: The Belltrees homestead. *Wesley Stacey.*

Right: Centre hallway and staircase at "Belltrees". *Wesley Stacey.*

this homestead today is regarded as opulent, in 1906 it was built for utilitarian purposes. There had to be the usual living area as well as a large pantry, kitchen, scullery, laundry and staff quarters. The plans selected included 52 rooms, measuring 151½ squares, not including 57 squares of verandah as an insulation from the heat.[5]

Mr. W. H. Noad of East Maitland was appointed contractor and Mr. John Taylor, clerk of works. Both were supervised by the architect Pender, who had been instructed to keep expenses within the realm of £11,000. The house took eighteen months to build and by October 25, 1908 the H. L. White family, along with Ernest and Victor, moved into their new homestead. On that day, "H. L." wrote to the architect as follows:

> ". . . we made a move into the new place yesterday but are in a bit of a muddle. I wish Noad would fix up the gas leak . . ."[6]

"H. L." spoke highly of both Noad and Taylor and thought them attentive to their work and very particular in the way everything was carried out. The only hold-ups were due to the difficulty in securing and keeping skilled workmen. The wage of a carpenter in 1907 was 1/3p. an hour for a forty-eight hour week. The quality of workmanship is manifest today in the homestead. The joinery is of a high standard particularly the detail of the main staircase which is carved from Richmond River cedar. The Wunderlich ceilings are still in perfect condition nearly seventy-five years later, all bearing the original paintwork of three tones of beige and ivory, highlighted by silver-leaf.

"H. L." ordered the new furniture from the firm Beard Watson's in Sydney. It was ready to arrive on June 10, 1908 so he instructed Beard Watson's as follows:

> "I wish to bring all your stuff from Morpeth (near Maitland) and in order to make it worth the carriers' while to go there, I have to supply loading to the port. At present I have some 30 tons of wool to send away, so should like you to forward an equal weight to meet my wool teams at Morpeth."[7]

Homestead garden in 1908, the year the family moved houses. *Sid Jackson.*

The dining room in the Arthur White's home "Kioto" 1892. *J. Check.*

their new homestead. Victor married Ruth Withycombe in 1910 and decided to move to "Lulworth", Darlinghurst in Sydney, presently the site of St. Luke's Hospital. In 1914, Ernest died suddenly from a burst appendix, leaving "H. L." and Louisa Maude the new large residence to themselves.

There were two rooms in the new homestead that "H. L." liked best — the billiard room, where his curator, S. W. Jackson, was kept occupied; and the library, where "H. L." would retire after dinner and write his numerous letters. From 1899 onwards, "H. L." had been encouraged by A. H. Spencer of Angus and Robertson to collect rare Australian books on voyages, explorations, natural history, anthropology, poetry and Australia in general. The books that he collected over the years were displayed in special cases made of Queensland maple and these lined the four walls of his library as they do today. Unfortunately, the H. L. White collection of Australian books was to suffer a different fate from that of the two collections bequeathed to the nation. These remained intact while the library, through sheer economic necessity, has been split up. As a result, it is difficult to estimate the magnitude of the H. L. White Library. Many of the books were sold upon his death in 1927 in order to defray death duties. In 1978, when cattle prices plummeted, a further selection of books was dispersed through Sydney Antiquarian booksellers, Timothy and Anne McCormick. In my pursuit of knowledge about the collection, I sought assistance from Timothy McCormick who has remarked:

> "It is to be regretted that the catalogue of the fine library of H. L. White has long since been lost; but with careful examination of the remaining books, noting their shelf numbers, it can be assumed that the collection consisted of approximately 2,500 volumes. H. L. White's interests, as reflected in his books, ranged from the early voyages of the discovery of the South Seas by Dampier, through Cook's epic travel, to the accounts of the First Fleet and the ultimate settlement at Port Jackson. From here H. L. White acquired all the major (and many ephemeral) rarities associated with the early years in the colony, together with the discovery and development of the inland. Without exception, all the journals of

thropology and inter-relationship with the white colonists formed a significant sub-collection with all the standard authors and texts being represented.

Of course, natural history was the feature, John Gould's magnificent *Birds of Australia* with the supplement, being the 'plum'. Gould's other works on the mammals and kangaroos also featured as did Mathews' 'monograph' and that primary ornithological work by J. W. Lewin *The Birds of N. S. W.* All other disciples of natural history were equally present including work by naturalists such as McCoy and Krefft.

A separate Philatelic Library of some 150 volumes established another feature of his notable collection.

Although the individual authors are not known today, it may be assumed that this part of the collection equalled the rest in quality, especially when viewing it together with H. L. White's unsurpassed collection of Australian stamps. All books present, without exception, were in excellent condition, great care being shown in the selection of copies. Any volumes with defective bindings were refurbished or, where necessary, rebound to high standards, usually by the firm of Morrells in London . . ."[8]

In 1916, H. L. White made a list of 400 volumes for valuation by Angus and Robertson — these comprising only a portion of his library. The valuation then was £710.

Tim McCormick has said:

"Today they would value at approximately $150,000. An informed guess as to the whole library of H. L. White during his life time, if it remained intact, would be in the region of $300,000."[9]

It was ironical that when part of the H. L. White library was dispersed in 1929, it was Albert Spencer, the man who had helped "H. L." acquire the numerous rare books on Australiana, who disposed of them. Spencer had admired "H. L." throughout all their negotiations and it was to him that he turned in 1922 when he wanted to leave Angus and Robertson in Sydney and set up his own bookshop, "The Hill of Content". In his own book titled *Hill*

needed. Spencer says:

> "This was typical of him. If you had his trust there was no need for security . . . as "H. L." left to go, his last words were 'try not to lose it, but if you do your best and fail, and lose this money, try not to think too much about it.' "[10]

Three years later, Mr. Spencer paid back the money plus interest. Understanding the nature of men, H. L. White accepted the repayment, not through need but rather through his knowledge that no man wants to base the success of his business on charity. "The Hill of Content" bookshop thrived and was highly esteemed by many in the realm of rare books.

H. L. White taught other people to appreciate good books and to read good books. Not only did he give £1,000 to the Royal Ornithological Union of Australia in Melbourne for a club room for members, but also he donated to the Union the complete set of John Gould's *Birds of Australia* as well as twelve volumes of Mathews' work. Each book in the H. L. White collection bore his ex libris book plate, designed for him by Lionel Lindsay, one of the famous Lindsay brothers. Even today, fifty years after the library's dispersal, I am often shown a rare Australiana book by friends whose libraries carry volumes with the H. L. White ex libris.

As Tim McCormick concludes:

> "The pleasure which the acquiring of each volume gave to H. L. White was given again to new collectors and so it is until this day, when bibliophiles are still proud to own a book emanating from this splendid collection."[11]

So life within the new "Belltrees" homestead during the H. L. White era was much more vocational than social. Through all the activity generated by "H. L.", the women were left to hibernate indoors and wile away the daylight hours. The Ebsworth sisters disliked sunshine and either sheltered behind blinds or, when venturing outside, wore large wide-brimmed hats, with long black skirts and lace blouses held together with a silver-buckled belt. There were domestic staff to assist them and it's difficult today to imagine what such women did other than knit, sew and play croquet.

The Ex-Libris or bookplate of H. L. White by Lionel Lindsay.

Left: "Boiling the billy" by the Hunter River. Louisa Maude White with her two daughters Dorothy and Norah.

Right: Matron Allen (centre) and some Scone hospital staff after afternoon tea at "Belltrees". Oct. 28, 1924. *H. L. White.*

Louisa Maude, after the birth of her son, was never a well woman. She was not strong and suffered constant ill health. "H. L." shouldered the responsibility of managing household staff problems and it was he who hired and fired. The problems were constant. The employment agencies in Sydney often sent incompetent people to help. One cook who was sent had the sole credential of peeling potatoes on a trip out from England, while other servants soon realised how isolated the place was and returned to the city. To maintain perfection under these conditions was no easy task.

H. L. White did not enjoy entertaining. His visitors were either ornithological friends or members of his own family. A reading of the Visitors' book of "Belltrees" from that time highlights the distinguished list of ornithological names who visited "Belltrees" — Lancelot Harrison; Captain S. A. White; A. J. Campbell; D. Le Souef; J. P. Austin; G. M. Mathews; A. G. Bassett-Hull; G. A. Waterhouse; Neville Cayley; Dr. J. A. Leach, and Alex Chisholm.

H. L. White's two daughters, Dorothy and Norah were married at "Belltrees", Dorothy to William Percival Minell and Norah to the famous "googly" bowler H. V. Hordern. The grandchildren often visited and stayed at "Belltrees". Dorothy's son, Bruce Minell, told me that he loved coming to "Belltrees" as a small boy; he always felt welcome but he was only allowed to move within certain rooms in the house. The study (or library) and the music room (or sitting room) were out of bounds and the

Louisa Maude was a tall, distinguished looking woman with rimless spectacles which gave her a rather severe, dour countenance although her nature was essentially gentle and kind. In all the family records she receives slight attention. Her presence seems to have been taken for granted but she was sadly missed, especially by "H. L.", if she left "Belltrees" during the hot summer months to rest at her seaside home at Terrigal. Whilst at "Belltrees", Mrs. "H. L." enjoyed her drives in her Nash or Hudson cars. "H. L." had gone to great trouble to import a special car for her. He wanted a dark green one but the first he ordered caught fire on ship on the way to Australia. Eventually it was replaced by one which bore Mrs. "H. L.'s" initials on the door. The entrusted chauffeur, Win Thrift, would take Mrs. "H. L." for drives in the afternoon. She was very fond of her sisters, Mrs. James White of "Edinglassie" and Mrs. Arthur White of "Kioto" and would often visit them for afternoon tea.

Louisa Maude enjoyed having her sister, Millicent, on "Belltrees" with her and that was not difficult since "Kioto" was only half a mile away. Millicent and Arthur White had decided on the site to build their house because it was an old cattle camp and "A. G." thought the stock knew best where the coolest place in the summer was, and the warmest spot in the winter, so he laid the foundations for his future home at the foot of a conical hill protecting him from hot westerly winds. Since she had no children of her own, Mrs. A. G. White was well known as "Aunt Millie" and "Aunt Millie" enjoyed painting. One day I was delighted to find a painting of hers in the old carpentry shop. I had it restored and reframed. She had obviously started to paint it while overseas as it has a great "Constable" touch with dark feathery trees in the foreground. But she must have completed her artwork when she returned home, for the background is a shower of rain falling on a wide Australian panorama. In the photograph of the dining room (pg. 102), it is this painting which is above the mantlepiece. It is a favourite of my daughter, Wendy, and it now hangs in her room in the homestead.

On cooler afternoons, guests were welcome in the garden. Mrs. "H. L." frequently had the sisters from the Scone Hospital

Mr. and Mrs. H. L. White preferred people to come for the day rather than to stay. But in 1919, the State Governor, Sir Walter Davidson and Lady Davidson paid a visit to the Scone district and were invited to stay at "Belltrees". "H. L." feared the event but was delighted afterwards with the couple whom he found very easy "for they spent three hours in the billiard room looking at my bird egg collection."[12] One of the highlights of Mrs. "H. L.'s" year was May 24, Empire Day, the birthday of Queen Victoria. Although Queen Victoria had been dead for over twenty years this day was patriotically remembered in this small outpost of the Commonwealth. Sometimes Mrs. "H. L." would organise a fête and bedeck the homestead lawn with flags of many nations. Sometimes a sports day was arranged on the sportsground. Whatever was decided, May 24 was a day set aside for everyone on the station to enjoy — there was plenty of food, tea and cool drinks for parents and for children. For Mrs. "H. L.", Empire Day was a ritual.

The picture which emerges is one of "H. L.", busy with his numerous interests — his property and all that it entailed as well as his collections of birds' eggs, bird skins, stamps and rare books; and Louisa Maude, uncomplainingly suffering her own illness and the preoccupation of her husband with all the demands that were made on his time. I find it difficult to capture the mood of the "Belltrees" homestead during this era — servants moving silently from room to room pulling the curtains to protect the women from the afternoon sun; few outsiders to disturb the peace; a general tone of quiet and a subdued but serene atmosphere. Recently, I lifted an old piano stool in the homestead and saw a leather bound book, "Louisa Maude Ebsworth - Music". It was "The Opera Bouquet - Twelve Operatic Fantasias arranged for one Piano by Immanuel Liebach".

Perhaps it was Mrs. "H. L.'s" piano and the strains of classical music which compensated her for many hours of solitude.

"Empire Day was a ritual". Tug of war.

Aerial view of homestead.

H. L. WHITE'S SCIENTIFIC INCLINATIONS not only permeated life at the homestead but also they manifested themselves in life on the property. The flower gardens, the lawns and the trees were of no less importance to him than the birds which inhabited them. He experimented with new varieties of fruit in the orchard and cultivated experimental plots of vegetables and crops. It was easy to find prize chrysanthemums in the gardens; figs, grapes, oranges, apples, walnuts, almonds and peaches in the orchard; and, in the vegetable garden, cauliflowers, turnips and pumpkins which went by cartload to the Scone markets after the employees had had their share.

"H. L." also worked with William Farrar in the development of a rust resistant type of wheat. To this end, there was an experimental plot on "Belltrees" and eventually the new type enabled northern New South Wales farmers to greatly increase their yields. "H. L." also dabbled in cotton growing; and Gus Collinson, whose descendants remain today a well known Hunter Valley family, rented the "Junction" paddock and grew tobacco there for many years. Bob Leggett, who worked on "Belltrees" as a full time farmer, tried to grow skinless barley and developed a new hybrid of maize known as "Leggett's Pride" which won an award at an agricultural exhibition at Wembley in England, thereby bringing international credit to the "Belltrees" farming projects.

"H. L." knew that for all this a knowledge of water resources was essential. He and his elder brother, James Cobb White, were talented water diviners and were often prevailed upon by friends and neighbours to find sites for wells. "H. L."

surrounded by a high wire fence, the "Kangaroo paddock", in which he kept thirty different types of kangaroo, wallaroo and wallaby. "H. L." detested cats and a cat-trap was always set on the big lawn to protect the visiting birds. Beside his office he had a large cage made to house an injured, rare, white goshawk; another cage for a pet crow who would imitate "H. L.'s" voice and call "Bill, Bill" to the gardener who, thinking it was "the boss", would come running. Beside this cage was a white eagle. This rare albino was later given to Taronga Park Zoo where it lived for many years eyeing the public.

"H. L.'s" interest in plant life absorbed him as much as his birds, his stamps and his books. He realised that the success of any pastoral pursuit is dependent upon the nutritional value of grasses. He analysed the types of natural grasses on the property in the hope of fostering those of high food value and preventing the spread of weeds or grasses of low nutritional worth. He collected forty-six different species of grass upon "Belltrees" and had each one analysed and catalogued and put into a reference collection housed in a large glass cabinet. This he donated to the Upper Hunter Pastures Protection Board in 1920. Accompanying the cabinet is a book *Key to the Collection of Grasses and Herbs* in which each page is ruled and recorded according to the scientific name of the grass, the vérnacular name, the original habitat and the feeding value. In this analysis "H. L." was ably assisted by his friend, J. H. Maiden, Curator of the Botanical Gardens in Sydney. Maiden was an incredible man who worked arduously and willingly to help people in their pursuit of botanical knowledge. The poor man must have dreaded the mail arriving on his desk bearing the "Belltrees" postmark for these were the sorts of items that fell out of the packets:

"Dear Sir,
By this mail I am forwarding to you for identification some scrub fruits, leaves and their bark, also a fungi, the latter having been

Mr. J. H. Maiden.
Courtesy Mitchell Library.

Or, on August 13, 1912:

"Dear Sir,
I send per same mail samples of berries which have passed through the native bird Strepra graculine and those picked from the tree. Would an analysis show what property has been used by the bird . . . as far as I can judge there is no difference between the eaten and uneaten berries . . . do you know anyone who will report upon contents of bird's stomachs for me?

H. L. White."[2]

Perhaps J. H. Maiden forgave "H. L." because Maiden too possessed an inquiring mind and was only satisfied when an object was correctly identified and clearly labelled. In the same letter as the above, "H. L." describes a hybrid wattle grown at "Belltrees" that he thought merited a new species. And it was a new species which Maiden named "Acacia H. L. White". It is the first authentic record of a cross-bred wattle having flowered. "H. L." collected a sample from his wattle tree and pressed it neatly into a frame on July 28, 1913. This still hangs in a room in the homestead while the actual acacia trees line the road from the gardener's cottage at the bottom of the "Belltrees" garden to the office.

J. H. Maiden was the Government Botanist in Sydney for twenty-five years. He was a well-loved personality, as patient with H. L. White as he was with all his botanical friends and staff. "H. L.'s" admiration of Maiden had started early in his managerial career. When "H. L." first took over "Belltrees" in 1885, one of his prime concerns was for the eradication of prickly pear. He realised the problem, together with the expense of getting rid of it. J. H. Maiden had written numerous articles warning the settlers of this pest but unfortunately the prickly pear originated in the Scone district.

Dr. W. B. Carlyle had carefully brought the first cactus plant from India and thought it would cultivate easily and form a nice protective hedge around Satur and Invermein in Scone. The fruit by birds and foxes, had taken over 60 million acres of good grazing land in northern New South Wales and Queensland and formed impenetrable jungles in which even trees died.[3]

It was not until later when the Government imported large numbers of its natural parasite, the cactoblastic moth from South America, that the rapid spread of prickly pear was brought under control. Prior to this date, the Whites had doggedly struggled on and continued to employ "pear gangs" on "Belltrees" in an attempt to overcome the pest, despite the fact that the operation was timely and costly.

H. L. White relied heavily on the botanical advice of J. H. Maiden. When Maiden retired in 1925 from his position of Government Botanist, he ended his farewell address thus:

> ". . . I have never willingly humbugged a man in my life. I have tried to do my best for you all and I never told you a lie . . ."[4]

Would that we all could boast such an epitaph.

Nancy Gray of the Scone Historical Society told me that "H. L." used to encourage the local shire workers to propagate native shrubs along the roadways. He instructed them to cover a native plant, gather the pod or seeds and replant them — a refreshing incentive to beautify the district and relieve the monotony of constant road maintenance.

To H. L. White, collecting was a function of being a successful pastoralist. He knew that without proper pastures his herd would necessarily suffer. Botanical species that he selected were used for propagation and upgrading. Likewise, he analysed any insects and pests that he collected. If he learned anything new within the district that would be beneficial to other pastoralists, he placed an article in the local newspaper. He loved to interest employees and children in the value of natural science. Bob Sutherland, as a schoolboy of ten, found an interesting insect that he knew "H. L."

fact. The female you sent is apparently full of eggs. She lives entirely on leaves and has a very wide range from Tasmania to New Guinea.

Thanks for sending the Spiny Green Leaf insect. I am always glad to help young people in the study of natural history.

I return the amount of the stamp, threepence halfpenny, that you had to put on the packet.

Yours faithfully,
H. L. White.
16/3/1922."[5]

Such a letter demonstrates that behind the disciplined exterior, there dwelt a generous spirit.

In the course of performing his everyday duties in the management of "Belltrees", "H. L." would analyse the value of grasses and trees, the destruction of pests and the habits of numerous creatures. He collected any rare species he saw and was interested in all that nature produced. More scientifically, he wanted to know how and why She produced it. He once wrote to a friend, "You must have a hobby in the bush . . . it is a relief from the sheep, cattle and dog talk . . ."[6] Yet, sheep and cattle were his lifeblood, the vehicles through which profits could be made and hobbies enjoyed.

Consistent with his outlook, "H. L.'s" sheep and cattle had to be of the highest standard and possess hybrid vigor. He approached his breeding programme in a scientific manner. Sheep farming had been the major primary industry undertaken by the early owners of "Belltrees" and by the time "H. L." became manager in 1885, the flock had increased dramatically. The "Belltrees" wool clip was highly regarded, as "H. L.'s" uncle, Henry Charles White, was a geneticist of note who had upgraded the "Belltrees" flock.

H. C. White held in great respect Nicholas Paget Bayly who had crossed English rams with German ewes and in this way evolved a flock known as the "Havilah" bloodline. H. C. White introduced this strain of sheep to "Belltrees" in the 1860's. Not only did H. C. White bring the 'Havilah" sheep bloodline to

"Belltrees" to be shorn for it was easier to bring them through the many crossings of the Hunter River rather than risk the wool waggon being bogged. Stockmen would leave the station at "Belltrees" with shorn sheep and exchange them with the woolly sheep being brought down from "Ellerston". "H. L." used to go personally to "Ellerston" to cull out all the rams, ewes and wethers. Alec Wiseman, still on "Belltrees" today, and Hunter Cobb, now a resident in Scone, were allowed to learn as small boys by standing alongside "the boss". However, in 1924 the "Ellerston" portion of "Belltrees" was sold — 20,000 acres to Mr. L. W. Friend of Quirindi and so was relinquised a portion of the estate that had been in the White hands since 1854. But the problems of management were becoming excessive and had to be countered. Yet, with "Ellerston" now gone, the "Belltrees" wool clip dropped dramatically and the emphasis turned to more beef cattle production. By the end of the 1920's, a large herd roamed the "Belltrees" grasslands. They were Aberdeen Angus cattle also upgraded through a cross-breeding programme.

Originally, when "H. L.'s" father, Francis, and his two brothers came to "Belltrees", they brought with them Durham (Shorthorn) cattle from "Edinglassie". This original Shorthorn stud was one of the oldest in New South Wales and used bulls from "Warrah" and "Bylong" studs up until 1889. In that year, H. E. A. & V. White made a large purchase of pure-bred heifers from another White property, "Martindale" stud. These heifers were of the celebrated "Border Chief" strain, mostly red in colour. H. E. A. & V. White decided from then on to use nothing but red bulls and in 1908 two of "H. L.'s" brothers toured Great Britain in search of them. However, previously, in 1897, "the firm" had purchased many high class Angus bulls from D. G. Clark of Gippsland.[7] Nonetheless, by 1919, 90% of "Belltrees" cattle were still dark red. But when a deterioration occurred in the colour of the Shorthorn herd, it became necessary to cross it with Angus bulls in order to maintain the standard of bullocks required for market. This upgrading programme proved a success with the result that "the firm" purchased stud Angus cows and top bulls

Opposite: Shedhands at work in the "Belltrees" shearing shed 1901. The poem was written by a Belltrees shearer c. 1910. *Courtesy Mrs. C. Rossington.*

The shearing is commencing and the boys are rolling up,
They are coming from afar, good tallys for to cut.
For hear their songs aringing through those
lovely hills and dales,
'Twould make your heart rejoice to think of coming days.

Now the shearing has commenced and the boys
are in full swing,
The echo of the tar boys voice, above all others ring.
Mr. McFadyn walks the shearing floor to see the sheep
are all well shore.
Then down you go right on the skin, no barcoo
cut will do for him.

Mr. McAtier stands classing all day, and Mr. Cobb Jnr.
polite visits pays.
Then Mr. White oft comes for a peep, to see the fine
wool come off his good sheep.
Mr. Cobb Snr. has all things correct, Sheep counted
quickly, the numbers well kept.
He manages well with surprising good style,
Which surpasses all stations for many a mile.
I've travelled the Darling and Lachlan as well,
For a home in my travels at Belltrees I'd dwell.

Those beautiful mountains and valleys so green,
Would make a home for an orphan,
or a sight for a Queen.

In the morning so early on those mountains so high,
To see the lambs playing 'twould fill you with joy.
The bright sunshine glitters, the birds sweetly sing,
To waken the slumbers of beautiful spring.

The musterer he rides through the run with
heart light and free,
to muster all sheep that he may see.
The night it comes on at the set of the sun,
he comes to the shed and his day's work is done.

The river runs close by the Belltrees homestead,
the breeze softly floats through the trees above head.
All is so green, so cheerful and gay,
As I stray by the river on a bright sunny day.

Farewell; to those rivers and valleys so green,
Farewell; to those hills where the playful lambs are seen.
Farewell; to the station and owner so kind,
Farewell; to the manager I must leave far behind.

with heavy stones and feeding the rough outside of the stack to the working bullocks. The inside of the stack he fed to mares and foals and cattle. Later, using a horse and scoop, a horse mower and hay waggon he pressed the green, cut feed into dirt pits dug into the ground. These ensilage pits were filled in good times and emptied when fodder was scarce. This system has been passed on from father to son and ensilage pits opened up after as many as twenty-five years in the ground have proved palatable for drought affected cattle.

On a property as big as "Belltrees", carrying such a large stock population, the movement of stock from paddock to paddock has been part of the daily life since the lands were fenced in the late 1830's. Inevitably, the value of a good horse was never underestimated and the Upper Hunter Valley topography of undulating hills and rugged ridges makes it essential that the horses be foot sure. The geology of this country is shale and limestone composition, ideal country for the breeding of thoroughbred or stock horses with strong bones. When the partnership of H. E. A. & V. White took over "Belltrees" in 1889 the Hon. James White gave his four nephews twenty high class fillies, the progeny of champions Chester and Martini-Henry. It was a generous bequest and these fillies were the foundation of the "Belltrees" horse stud.

The "Horse Book" at "Belltrees" has been meticulously compiled since 1888 and is still in current use. There are pedigrees and details of every horse bred on the place. Each year when the foals are branded, the year number is put over the stud book number and both are fired on the horse's ribs. The book records that 1,000 horses were branded on "Belltrees" up until 1891; a further 1,000 horses between 1891 and 1906; and another 1,000 from 1905 to 1915, making a total of 3,000 horses in all branded up until 1915.

The Hon. James White also gave his nephews Paraphrase which he had bred at "Kirkham", sired by his own stallion, Chester. Paraphrase had a tremendously strong breeding line,

Above: The two Belltrees bullock teams crossing the Hunter River at the Glen. 1905.

Right: A wool waggon bogged by getting off the road at Red Bank – Jump-Up Upper Hunter Road. 16 Nov. 1925. *H. L. White.*

Left: Belltrees tennis team en route to Gundy. Sept. 1919. *H. L. White.*

Right: Mrs. H. L. White (3rd from left) and friends at Randwick races (c. 1903).

being the dam of Parapet which won the famous Doncaster Handicap in Sydney in 1899. Parapet, in turn, was the grand dam of Melbourne Cup winner Bitalli. In fact, inspired by the earlier achievements of the Hon. James White, in 1896, H. E. A. & V. White provided the winner of the prestigous A. J. C. Derby — Charge, sired by the legendary Melbourne Cup winner Carbine. The victory ribbon is framed and today hangs in the homestead library. The Hon. James White had instructed his nephews, Henry, Ernest, Arthur and Victor, to treat horse breeding as a science and to pay attention to pedigree. By the turn of the century, the breeding and training of thoroughbreds on "Belltrees" was in its heyday. A racetrack was established at Echo Flat, below Arthur White's home "Kioto"; a horse trainer was kept in full-time employment along with six jockeys who lived on the station. The family's racing colours were originally gold, white hoops and a gold cap but in 1903 the A. J. C. changed the colours to yellow, white hoops and a yellow cap. Predictably, "H. L." wrote to the Victorian Racing Club informing them of the alteration in a letter depicting his fury.

Charge, the A. J. C. Derby winner, after two seasons at "Belltrees" stud was offered for sale in 1904 and Ruenalf became the chief stallion. In 1904, "Belltrees" mares were exported to Japan and the following year Ernest White attended a horse breeding conference in Sydney. Though not rivalling the successes of their uncle, the Hon. James White, "the firm" produced noteable winners of feature races on the New South Wales racing calendar. Golden Bronze, Golden Cello, Golden Curio and

V. White won four of the five races, three being won by the same horse, Andorra, a home bred two-year-old gelding by the "Belltrees" sire, Lennox. Ernest rode Andorra and then Rickshaw to win the Cup. The well-known reporter "Milroy" of the Sydney Mail wrote of the Picnic Races on May 26, 1900 that:

> ". . . Mr. Arthur White received the trophies on behalf of the Belltrees firm, and responded by thanking the President in the shortest speech on record . . ."[9]

Ernest died in 1914 but already plans were underway to disperse many of the "Belltrees" thoroughbreds. In February of that year "the firm" held a highly successful clearance sale. All the mares except a few special favourites were disposed of and a second sale was held a little more than a year later. Actually H. E. A. & V. White made a lucky move in disposing of the stud before the slump came. In 1915, "H. L." realised that "a fat bullock is worth as much as an average yearling".[10]

By the late 1920's, "the firm" had concluded several sales of surplus stock horse females and in this way the "Belltrees" bloodline was disseminated throughout the Valley.

The management of a large property; noteable and painstaking collections of bird skins, birds' eggs, stamps and books; scientific work in the field on grasses and pests; the breeding of stock and thoroughbreds; and the personal documentation of all of these offers us a picture of life at "Belltrees" then, as staggering in its dimension as it is in the quality of what was done.

This of course placed demands on the men but it must also have placed great strains on the women who were ill-prepared for the loneliness of such a life in rural Australia. In 1923, Louisa Maude White became very ill and was confined to hospital in Sydney. Her husband was distraught with worry. Her only son, "A. H.", then at Cambridge University in England, came back to visit her and "H. L." made as many trips to Sydney from "Belltrees" as was possible. However, as Victor was now living in Sydney permanently and Arthur was overseas, it was not practicable for "the boss" to leave "Belltrees" for long. In these

> ". . . Maude had held quite a levee and shook hands with everyone. Copious tears by some women who saw her for the first time in six months. . . ."[11]

"H. L." had part of the upstairs balcony glassed in so that his wife could convalesce at "Belltrees", but she did not stay there very long and would return with the nurses to her Terrigal house whenever she felt stronger. By 1924 "H. L." became excited at the thought of his son "A. H." returning home from England. Although suffering setbacks like an injured kneecap and a severe case of scarlet fever, "A. H.", whilst at Cambridge University, had excelled as a prominent cricketer. He was a fast bowler of great note and on August 23, 1924, "H. L." wrote of his son's cricket achievements to his egg collector in Western Australia, F. L. Whitlock:

> "My son's cricket has received favourable comment in English papers. He leaves shortly with the team to play against the Rhine Occupation Army; then to Ireland with an M. C. C. Eleven and afterwards to the United States of America with the University team; then home to Australia . . ."[12]

By November, 1924, "A. H." had returned to "Belltrees" and was put straight to work. "H. L." was delighted with his son and thought him:

> ". . . an intelligent, sensible, gentlemanly lad . . . very anxious to settle down and get to work. He was engaged the day after arrival here, at looking after the fire when cattle branding was on, a warm job for a new chum . . ."[13]

What "H. L." quite forgot was that his son or "the lad" was now twenty-three years old but nonetheless it was a joy to "the boss" to have him at "Belltrees" and to introduce him to the demands of management.

By the time "A. H." had returned, "Belltrees" was established as a successful pastoral enterprise but this only increased the day to day demands and it was a comfort to "H. L." to know that his son had returned to work on the land. In 1925 "H. L."

Group of Belltrees racehorses on racetrack, "Echo Flat". 1901.

"December 2nd, 1926
A cool pleasant day. Went to Scone with Nurse Crozier. Attended meeting of Shire Council for an hour and was elected President for 22nd consecutive term — a record for N.S.W. Rested for an hour at the Golden Fleece Hotel and returned home by 1.30 p.m."[15]

Gradually "H. L." became more feeble and he died in May, 1927. There was a short simple funeral service at Muswellbrook attended by many members of the White family from throughout New South Wales together with representatives from local organisations, state government departments and ornithological unions. Significantly, "H. L.'s" coffin was not borne by four members of his family or four dignitaries from Scone or Sydney. It was carried by four of his trusted employees from "Belltrees" — J. L. Greer, R. Leggett, A. Rose and W. Thrift.[16]

An era had ended.

When Alfred Henry Ebsworth White was born at "Belltrees" on October 18, 1901, his father, "H. L.", was so overcome with delight that he celebrated all evening. Next morning, he was unable to give the men orders so he turned to his head stockman, "Mitchell," he said, "give the men something to do." Then he ambled back up the lawn for breakfast. This was most unusual for "the boss" but now that he had produced an heir to the line of Whites at "Belltrees", his joy was apparent.

"H. L." was very proud of his son and tried to be a good father. But from the outset he sought to cast the boy in his own image, directing him to his hobbies when "A. H." was much more interested in shooting and cricket. Even "H. L." recognised this,

> "I took my small son with me to the England/Australia Test in 1911. Hordern presented him with a ball used in the match, after getting all the players to write their names on it. The kid would not change it for all my eggs."[1]

The ball bears an appropriate inscription recording that H. V. Hordern took twelve wickets for 175 runs in the Test. This was to prove a lasting inspiration to "A. H.", more so when two years later H. V. Hordern married "A. H.'s" sister, Norah.

"A.H." was only ten years old at the time of the Test but "H. L." already had him the youngest member ever, at eight, of the Australian Ornithological Union. Even when "A. H." returned home from Geelong Grammar during his holidays, "H. L." would

Master Alfred H. E. White of Belltrees Scone. Sept. 1909.
Youngest member of the Australian Ornithologists Union.
Courtesy National Museum of Victoria.

and attention that his Victorian childhood denied him. When he first went away to boarding school, "H. L." wrote to the Master, Mr. Austin, at Geelong Grammar about his son:

> "The lack of self-esteem if I may term the failing by such a name, is hereditary, I am afraid; my father publicly known as 'honest Frank White', although forced into public life was a shy reserved man . . . Alf possesses the family failing (his mother being of the reserved sort also) besides being spoilt as a child. For many years he was a very fragile, delicate little chap, and allowed therefore to take things easily. I used to have hopes of making something of him, an engineer from choice but am afraid that on the land must be his portion."[2]

"A. H." did well at Geelong Grammar School. Cricket was his primary interest and in this he starred. In 1915, he recorded remarkable success playing in the Under Fifteen team for Geelong Grammar. The school magazine of the day records his performances in this way:

- Versus Geelong College. Lost by 37. A. H. White, 7 wickets for 17 runs.
- Versus Geelong College (return match). Won by 44. A. H. White, 5 wickets for 4 runs.
- Versus Melbourne Grammar School. Lost by 9 runs. A. H. White, 8 wickets for 15 runs.[3]

Three inscribed cricket balls, now part of the White memorabilia in the homestead, record some of "A. H.'s" achievements while playing for the Geelong Grammar First Eleven: 8 for 14 against Xavier College on March 12, 1920; a week later, 7 for 20 against Melbourne Grammar; and a year later, a hat trick against Wesley College. The Geelong Grammar School magazine, *The Corian*, makes mention of A. H. White the cricketer. It recalls:

> ". . . White's great performance of 28 wickets for 120 runs calls for special comment. He bowled at a great pace with exceptional

of finishing. His fielding, especially at mid-off and cover, is finished and his return to the wicket, always accurate and quick."[4]

A. H. White was at school during World War I and even though he wanted to enlist, his father would not allow him to put his age up one year so he stayed on at Geelong Grammar until 1921. He was an intelligent and religious person who received the divinity prize at school and had a rare general knowledge of world geography. He was captain of cricket for four years and senior prefect for two terms before going to Jesus College, Cambridge. By this time he was something of a cricket name and in 1924 played for Cambridge University against South Africa, taking three vital wickets for 30 runs. In an important 9th wicket stand with Bagnall, he added 67 runs in thirty-eight minutes and remained 53 not out. After this match, and to his intense pride, "A. H." was awarded his cricket blue. Subsequently, he was hampered by injury but on his return home was selected on one occasion to represent New South Wales.

"A. H.", from early on, developed a close affinity with his mother who adored him and tended to spoil him. When Louisa Maude became very ill in 1923, "A. H." was so worried that he came home to Australia to see her. In those days it was quite a trip, overland to India and then boat to Australia. He finally returned to "Belltrees" in 1924 and in May, 1926 announced his engagement to Judy Lorna Coombe of Perth, Western Australia. "A. H." and Judy Lorna Coombe had met as school children on the same train going to Melbourne and again at the Hyde Park Hotel in London in 1924. She was a beautiful debutante of the Sydney scene, with a feminine, pretty face, blue eyes and blond hair. She was admired by many men, but it was always the aloof farmer from "Belltrees" who captured her attention. Upon the announcement of the engagement, "H. L." wrote to Miss Coombe:

> "Allow me to offer my congratulations. You will find Alf rather hard to manage; but will get him properly trained in time no doubt."[5]

Judy Lorna White. Portrait in oil by Judy Cassab 1965.

A. H. White. Portrait in oil, painted posthumously, by Paul Fitzgerald 1965.

Many prize ribbons for "Belltrees" cattle and horses, hang in the billiard room. *Max Easton*.

Judy Coombe were married in Sydney on September 20, 1926, but regrettably "H. L." was not well enough to attend the wedding of his only son. When "H. L." died in May, 1927, the total responsibility fell onto the young shoulders of A. H. White. He was then twenty-six, a diligent worker and a perfectionist — a workaholic. He devoted his entire life and energy to seeking perfection on "Belltrees".

It was not an easy period for Australia with this country and most of the world plunged into depression. "A. H." responded by employing cheap and willing labour. He replaced the old post and rail fences that surrounded "Belltrees" with wire and strong strainer posts. He was an astute manager but lacked tolerance. He would often go straight into some scheme without seeking advice. For example, one day he decided "that sheep were noxious like rabbits" and sold the entire flock. But at other times he was a hard traditionalist incapable of adapting to change. He insisted on standards being maintained at a time when it was becoming more difficult to maintain them. While he was regarded as a just man, in order to enforce his ideas he often became rather dictatorial rejecting objections or criticism. He could not suffer fools gladly. Everyone rather feared him, yet from his friends and family he won great respect. In many ways, "A. H." was his own worst enemy. He hid behind a thick facade of shyness and presented a frightening countenance which belied a gentle nature.

H. L. White had left his interest in "Belltrees" to his son "A. H." alone. Louisa Maude was still alive and to her he left a half share in the homestead for the rest of her lifetime. However, after "H. L." died, Louisa Maude moved permanently to Terrigal. At the same time, "H. L.'s" brother, Arthur White, who still retained a half share in the stock and land at "Belltrees" decided to keep his interests but move from his home "Kioto" and live in the Hotel Australia in Sydney. This left Mr. and Mrs. A. H. White in control of both the big "Belltrees" homestead and the smaller house, "Kioto". For a newly-married couple, the fifty-two room homestead was a daunting prospect, so Mr. and Mrs. "A. H." decided to live at "Kioto". In February, 1928 a son was born to them and a photograph later appeared in a Sydney paper headed,

"Residents of the Upper Hunter — in grateful remembrance of their benevolence and kindliness of heart."

After the first son, Mr. and Mrs. "A. H." then had three daughters, Morna born 1930; Bettine born 1932 and Primrose born in 1936. Michael was eight years old when Primrose was born at "Kioto" and remembers the day well:

> "Dad took me out into the paddocks in his utility truck. I was thrilled because he didn't take me out with him very often and when we returned to the house there was Prim squealing in her cot."

At this time, "A. H." made extensive alterations at "Kioto" to accommodate his children, employing for this purpose, first in 1930 and again in 1933, the builder John Taylor who had worked previously as a young man on the construction of the main homestead. However, during the depression, building materials were difficult to obtain so "A. H." pulled down the whole kitchen block of the "Belltrees" homestead, and cleaned the old sandstock bricks in order to put up the large nursery wing in his new house. As well, he built himself a large library at the end of the verandah and transferred all the library cabinets and books from the homestead. Reg Prevost, an architect and friend from Sydney, was commissioned to build a swimming pool in 1929, decidedly forward thinking for that era. There was a staff wing and staff to help at "Kioto". The three Greer girls, Florence, Annie and Mary helped Judy Lorna White with the cooking, the children and the laundry. Charlie Harman continued to work in the garden; Walter Storrier was "A. H.'s" valet; and a cowboy, Claude Ellery, attended to the milking, fowls, wood and boot cleaning.

The White children were brought up strictly. "A. H." tried to carry his own childhood image into a changing world a generation later. Michael, Morna, Bettine and Primrose lived with their nurse in the nursery wing and were seldom allowed across the courtyard

The "Kioto" homestead and rose garden in the 1930s.

Left: Mrs. A. H. White and her son, Michael Francis. *Cazneaux.*

Right: Michael and two of his sisters, Morna and Bettine. *Cazneaux.*

into the house. If they went into the kitchen they were punished. As a treat, some nights when "A. H." called out "action stations" the children were permitted into the dining room to sit quietly in the corner and watch their parents eat. One evening, Judy Lorna White turned to her husband and asked, "Where is the top of the Edam Cheese?" A voice from the corner could bear it no longer and piped up, "Please Mum, the Bishop ate it last night." They were allowed to watch but never to be heard.

"A. H." mellowed in later years but when his children were small he was dictatorial to them as his father had been towards him. In 1933, Mr. and Mrs. A. H. White went to England and left the three children, Michael, Morna and Bettine in the charge of Nurse McPherson; and the management of "Belltrees" in the hands of Hunter Cobb. When in 1935, Michael's tutor, a Frenchman who always rode a bicycle, was mocked so badly by the jackeroos in the boarding house that he left, Michael was ushered off to Tudor House, Moss Vale, at the age of seven. He longed to attend the "Belltrees" Public School but it was not his parents' wish.

By 1938, after ten years at "Kioto", "A. H.." decided to return to the "Belltrees" homestead. Much rebuilding had to be done as the whole kitchen block, as well as the ceilings and floors, interest in the vegetable garden. "Harmie" who worked for both men, was a genius at growing vegetables. "A. H." boasted fifty-four different varieties grown on the alluvial flat below "Kioto" and he would escort his lunch guests down the hill to inspect the project. Morna was eight years old when the family moved back to the homestead and she remembers her great-uncle Arthur coming up to stay at "Kioto". "I liked Uncle Arthur," she said recently. "As he was leaving to return to Sydney one day, he gave me a one pound note with instructions to share it with Michael, so I neatly tore it in half. I had never seen money before," she added.

When "A. H." inherited the management of "Belltrees", he immediately struck out on a large tidying-up campaign. He redid much of the fencing through the expert work of Albert Ward and his gang from Gundy — Bob Fogarty, Luke Cronin, Charlie Greer and Teddy Mitchell. "A. H.", with fewer employees, realised that there were numerous obsolete workmen's cottages on the property that, untidy and unused, should be demolished and cleared away. He had a passion for taking cartloads of rubbish to the tip. The family lived in dread that when he was undertaking a tidying-up campaign, something precious might end up in the gully. And so it did. For example, many of the children's favourite toys and blocks, as well as valuable ornithological data from his father's library, including early editions of the *Emu* Magazine of the R.A.O.U. went the way of the tip.

Yet "A. H." felt a great need to preserve the early Sempill buildings erected on "Belltrees". He employed Fred Jarvis in the late 1930's to restore the old slab store. Fred was a fencer and one of the best bush workers the station has known. He understood round timber and was brilliant with a mortising axe and adze. Fred replaced any individual posts whose butts had been rotted by floodwaters. It took him four years to restore the old slab store. When he had finished this job, he then replaced panels in the "Belltrees" stockyards using iron bark posts and rails for solidarity.

In the 1930's, "A. H." had jackeroos on "Belltrees" and they peacefully in the midday sun. Jim crept up stealthily to one of them and went "brrr...h". The bullock opened his eyes, got a fright, and dropped dead at Jim's feet. Speechless, poor Jim had to return to the station to report to "the boss" exactly what had happened.

Many of these jackeroos went off to World War II and tragically Jack Broughton and Jim Bullmore were killed in action in Europe. A bronze plaque to each of them has been erected in the "Belltrees" Chapel.

After World War II, "Belltrees", with its improvements, was an obvious take-over target for the government seeking to administer its Soldiers' Settlement Scheme. The estate had numerous houses, was well fenced and well watered, a "sitting-duck" to be neatly carved up. In 1946, the surveyor from Muswellbrook, Marcus Hyndes, a friend of "A. H." who had revered the work of his fellow surveyor, "H. L.", wanted to prevent this from happening. He made two proposals to "A. H." The first was to get on side with the government and, under the Voluntary Promotions Scheme, offer 12,000 acres of "Belltrees" at give-away prices to the Closer Settlement Board. The second proposal was to divide immediately the remaining vast acreage amongst members of the family so that the whole lot would not be in the names of A. H. and A. G. White alone. "A. H." adhered to this sound advice and acted promptly. He selected four local returned soldiers whom he knew and trusted to look after their land — his cousin, Herbert Hordern, Neil Cameron, Ian MacCallum and Bill Holmes. 12,000 acres in the Donald's Creek and Brushy Hill area were subdivided into 3,000 acre lots and became economic propositions and worthwhile properties, "Yeovil", "Oakendale", "Ardroy" and "Mandalea". Likewise, he split the rest of the estate into five liveable areas of 3,000 acres, each with a house. Michael received the Uri Block; Morna, the Stewart's Brook Block; Bettine, "Belltrees Farm"; Primrose, Woolooma Gully and the Lapstone Block; whilst "A. H." had the River paddock, the New paddock and the Homestead Block of 23 acres. He formed "Belltrees Grazing Company" as owner of the governments implement such schemes, to first understand the viability of the land they resume and subdivide.

Having completed all these transactions, "A. H." then realised that his Uncle Arthur, A. G. White, had made no provision for his half share of "Belltrees" should he die. The old uncle was now 84, living comfortably at the Hotel Australia in Sydney and very benevolent to The King's School, Cranbrook School, The Church of England and The Salvation Army. "A. H." went to visit him and explained that he did not wish to manage "Belltrees" in the future for charity. Uncle Arthur saw the rationality of that remark and when he died two years later in 1948, he kindly left his half share in the "Belltrees" estate in trust for "A. H.'s" four children — Michael, Morna, Bettine and Primrose. Subsequent to his death, a window was unveiled in St. Andrew's Cathedral, Sydney, in memory of Arthur White.

A. H. White decided to maintain the firm's name as "H. E. A. & V. White" and now was in a position to get on with the management of the station as a complete project. During World War II, faced with a critical labour shortage, "A. H." had sold the entire sheep flock. But by 1952 he predicted the wool boom and bought 4,000 Toganmain merino ewes from the Robertson family, and "Belltrees" was back into wool production. He purchased "medium wool" rams from the Kater brothers of "Mumblebone", Warren, and had Harry O'Brien come each year to class the flock. Gradually, the sheep numbers increased.

"A. H." was also interested in upgrading the Angus cattle herd. At different times during the 1930s, "A. H." bought six cows from Scotland, six from the "Waiterenui" stud, New Zealand; and five, including two heifers, from the renowned "Juana Erica" strain from Scotland. These shipments came to Scone by rail and were met by the local carrier, Roy French, who brought them to "Belltrees" by motor lorry. They were the first cattle to be delivered up the Valley by motor transport. In 1935, "A. H." went to New Zealand with his friend, Frank Bragg of "Rossgole", Aberdeen, to attend the dispersal sale of the Gwavas' Aberdeen Angus stud. At this sale, "A. H." purchased a further six more were sent from "Belltrees" to Japan, New Guinea, The Philippines, South Australia and many parts of Victoria and New South Wales. These cattle proved to do well wherever they went and buyers returned to "Belltrees" for repeat drafts. More Angus bulls, selected for size and quality, were then purchased from "Mangotoro", "Crickelwood", "Akitio" and "Turihaua" in New Zealand; and from the home studs of "Booroomooka", "Wallah", "Bald Blair", "Tulagi" and "Hazeldean" in New South Wales.

Likewise, although no thoroughbred race horses were being bred at "Belltrees", "A. H." concentrated on sound stock horses. In the 1930's, he had purchased a Cecil colt named Serene, who was from a Blanch mare bred by J. J. Mackay. This colt was put to stud and not only bred top stock horses used for campdrafting work but also it bred good polo ponies as well. As evidence of this, in the 1930's, two stockmen from "Belltrees" won two Australian championships — Alec Wiseman for campdrafting and Harry McPhee for roughriding. Throughout the following decade by using stallions such as Serene, which was renamed Wildfire, and Klimop, the pedigrees in the horse stud book at "Belltrees" were maintained.

1950 saw a period of great prosperity on the land in New South Wales in general and at "Belltrees" in particular. There was a wool boom, cattle prices were favourable and the seasons were good. "A. H." and his wife, Judy Lorna White, enjoyed many overseas trips to Honolulu and Europe, and sent two of their daughters to finishing school in Switzerland.

1952 became a turning point in A. H. White's life. His eldest daughter, Morna, asked her father if she may announce her engagement to be married. "A. H." then realised that his children were leaving home and he no longer had absolute control over them. Only now did he understand that the station work on "Belltrees" had dominated his life and he had allowed valuable time to slip away. He had been a difficult man in his own home, given to such outbursts of temper that his children were often in fear of him. It was his wife, Judy Lorna White, who calmed any

Aberdeen Angus cattle on "Belltrees". *David Moore. Time-Life Books.*

Judy Lorna made up genuine-sounding excuses. If they went for a drive in the rain, it was Mrs. White who opened the gates in the wet. With a rare willingness to please, Judy Lorna White sucumbed to "A. H.'s" every wish. But by 1952, the despotic camouflage of A. H. White had come adrift to reveal the true man who had been hidden by a strict and often frightening facade. He became much more approachable and allowed to emerge a softer nature that had been previously trapped by his outer image. Though it was not easy, more and more he learned to unwind.

It is in this same year that I met A. H. White for the first time. Instead of meeting the severe person many of my friends had frightened me with, I met a most interesting man. However, I do remember vividly my first visit to "Belltrees". Michael invited me to stay during the May university vacation. I had had a different childhood from that of the White children. My upbringing was rather carefree. I was very close to my mother and had mixed constantly with her friends, calling them by their christian names. For me, no generation gap existed. My first dinner at "Belltrees" with the whole White family, Mr. and Mrs. A. H. White, Michael, Morna, Bettine and Primrose, was memorable. As I entered the dining room, I was blinded by strong centre light. It was obvious that meals were functional and everybody had to see what they ate. Then having been taught to eat slowly and make one's conversation at dinner-time interesting, intelligent and entertaining, I was met by empty plates and silence. My plate was almost untouched as I had never drawn breath during my soliloquy. My mother had instructed me always to help when I was asked away to stay, so I got up and took out the plates returning into the dining room to remove all the salts and peppers from the table before the pudding was served. I noticed each member of the family look at one another, then at the salt and then at me. After dinner, everyone drifted off. Morna, Bettine and Primrose played canasta while I casually sauntered off to the warmest fire and joined "A. H." in his smoke room. The morning papers were all neatly rolled and shock to the White family as it had been to me. No one, I was told, of our generation had ever dared to talk so freely in the "Belltrees" dining room before.

Obviously, I was soon forgiven, for I received an invitation to attend the wedding at "Belltrees" of Morna White and David Hardy Playfair on September 20, 1952. The day before the wedding was another memorable experience. I was again staying at the homestead and although there were many preparations for the wedding, "A. H." realised that there was also station work that he wanted done. He could not bear to see anyone idle so he took the bridgegroom, David Playfair, Harry Evans and me into the No. 3 lucerne paddock to spray the variegated thistles. Michael and his father drove the spray truck while the three of us stood at intervals in the paddock to be markers so that the truck could be driven in a straight line. Everytime the spray truck passed us, we would take three paces forward in order to be next line marker when the truck turned. This operation went on for hours. Alone, in the centre of that lucerne paddock, I declared that I would never ever come and stay at "Belltrees" again. Fortunately, David and Harry were also getting restless as each of us was out of range of any conversation. So we decided to cheat and take four paces forward in order to quicken the performance. This helped us but we had outstepped the capacity of the spray's arms and had safely returned to Sydney when the healthy thistles grew in strips amid the dead ones. David Playfair subtly incorporated the "spraying" ordeal into his bridgegroom's speech next day and also mentioned the rigours of attempting to court a White daughter. He drew attention to the locked gates and to the heavy bands of chain that "A. H." used on purpose as an obstacle.

Within the next four years, "A. H.'s" other three children were married, Bettine to William Ross Chandler on June 13 1953; Michael to Judy Crossing on February 3, 1956; and Primrose to David Arnott on October 20, 1956. The three daughters were married in the "Belltrees" Chapel and the guests strolled across the paddock to the reception at the homestead. Each bride threw her bouquet from the balcony landing on the stairway; and at each

"A. H." loved sending cables. He was a proud grandfather and he obviously regarded the baby as a White first, forgetting that it was really a Playfair. Then in 1957, Michael and I had a son, Antony Alfred Luke. This was the first White grandson. Antony was born at 4.00 a.m. on the morning of January 18 and A. H. White was so ecstatic with the news that he decided to fire a 21 gun salute from the top balcony of the homestead in order to inform everybody of the event. Judy Lorna White stood beside him in her nightdress, quietly holding the hot barrel of one gun and reloading the other whilst "A. H." fired the salute.

The last decade of "A. H.'s" life was perhaps his happiest time. He allowed himself to reap the benefits of all he had worked for. "Belltrees" had reached a high standard of excellence. The buildings were in perfect upkeep, the fences immaculate and the stock in prime condition. "A. H." strove for perfection at the expense of everything else. He had achieved his aim and he could now delegate responsibility to his only son, Michael and leave "Belltrees" more often to enjoy other pleasures. Each winter, he and his wife would follow the sun and go to different islands on the Barrier Reef or to Honolulu, which they loved. Whilst at home, "A. H." spent many hours in his library, reading avidly. He admired American literature and bought many volumes telling "how the West was won." He admired the early Indian conquests and thought Australian history uneventful in comparison. Wyatt Earp, Simon Kenton and General Cutler were his heroes. He visited America often and came home to "Belltrees" with every new household gadget imaginable. Visiting America to him was, he felt, like discovering the New World.

A. H. White was a Director of Pitt Son & Badgery in Sydney whilst his friend, J. D. MacLeod was Chairman. The White family have had a long association with this well-known stock and station company and have relied heavily on the advice and organisation of such men as R. M. Pitt and J. D. MacLeod, and, in more recent times, Clair Levett and Alan Farrer. Michael became a Director

The Belltrees garden now has a parkland atmosphere. *Wesley Stacey*.

used to watch in adoration whilst the grandchildren performed little pranks that, if done thirty years ago by his own children, would have created a furore. But "A. H.'s" four children, Michael White, Morna Playfair, Bettine Chandler and Primrose Arnott, understood that their father had mellowed in later years; and they were pleased that the grandchildren were receiving the attention that they had been denied at the same age.

A. H. White died suddenly on March 6, 1964 in Sydney. He left his land, cattle and homestead in equal parts to his four children as the late Arthur White had also done. His son, Michael, became manager of "Belltrees". Like his sisters, he possessed the dominant trait of each parent — the strength of character of his father and the kindly nature of his mother. This invaluable combination has enabled any decisions that have had to be made between Michael and his three sisters to be transacted not for selfish gain, but rather with the well-being and perpetuity of "Belltrees" paramount in all their thoughts. I cannot make this last point forcibly enough because it is tragic throughout Australian rural history to see how many old family properties have been torn asunder by family friction. For five generations, the Whites have exercised a mutual understanding in family dealings. Perhaps this, more than anything else, has made it possible to preserve the "Belltrees" heritage.

on "Belltrees"

THE PERPETUATION OF A FAMILY HERITAGE is not easy. Not only does it require unselfishness and understanding amongst all members of the family which has created it; but just as vitally it demands a loyalty from staff and employees who are often the architects of its survival. Therefore, the history of "Belltrees" is not only the history of the White family but rather it encompasses the lives and contributions of many other people and other families.

In my study of the diaries and wage books of the "Belltrees" estate for the past 150 years, one of the distinguishing aspects has been the recurrence of the same names. While management and ownership have passed from father to son for six generations, so too, many of the tasks of everyday life on the station have been kept in the same name for generations whether it be the Rossingtons as blacksmiths, the McInnes family as stockmen or the Cobbs as station managers. And it has been the dedication, loyalty and plain hard work of many generations of employees that have contributed towards making "Belltrees" the heritage it is today.

It is difficult for the present day worker to comprehend the employee-employer relationship that existed between man and master in early rural life. There existed then a genuine concern for each other's needs and commitments and in many ways survival depended upon it. Transportation and communications were virtually non-existent making employment a permanent rather than a temporary state. The station's autonomy meant that outside agitation, when it did occur, failed to penetrate into the life of the take a pecuniary measurement and say that the rural workers of yesterday were badly off, for happiness in work, even today, is a better yardstick of satisfaction than material gain. The fact that so many families stayed on "Belltrees" for so long speaks for itself. It is a derivative of this attitude of pride in workmanship which was rare and undeniable. The men realised that their efforts built up the assets of the property and the station community so that another cottage could be built and maintained for someone's comfort; or an entertainment hall could be constructed where Saturday night films were shown for the benefit of everybody who came along.

The employees evidently respected the fact that the White family held their interests in high priority. The White men scorned carousing, lavish entertaining, the holding of balls or other outward expressions of wealth. Most of what they earned was re-invested back into the improvements on "Belltrees" — better land, better stock and better conditions for those who worked here. For example, in 1922, when A. H. White turned 21, Mr. and Mrs. "H. L." did not hold a ball to celebrate the event at the homestead. Instead, they preferred a special sport's day for all the employees and families on "Ellerston" and "Belltrees" with races for all including stepping races for the women and tug-of-war for the men. There were lashings of food and cool drink. At night, a dance was held in the entertainment hall and at the end of the party everyone (there were 250 in those days) formed into a single file, marched past the stage and received a present.

Though "A. H." was still at Cambridge University in England, everyone on "Belltrees" drank a toast to him and when the employees organised to send a cable from them to him, "H. L." was deeply touched. Likewise, at the end of World War II, when "A. H." held a celebration dinner, he had it in the courtyard at the back of the homestead so that everyone on the property could join with him. That practice lives on today with the annual station Christmas party for everybody on "Belltrees".

It is remarkable, if not unique, that at this present time,

Cecil McInnes shows Scott White how to preserve old harness for the "Belltrees" museum. *Ern McQuillan.*

Alec Wiseman.
Like all good bushmen he always
carries his pocket knife and wax matches. *Laurence Le Guay*.

George Mitchell, first child born on "Belltrees" (c. 1837).
Photo taken July, 1921 at the age of 83 years. *H. L. White.*

Today 1981, his descendant, George Mitchell, pressing wool in the original wool press.
Laurence Le Guay.

Mustering cattle along the river. *James Fitzpatrick.*

early as 1831. His son, also George, was the first child born at "Belltrees" and when he grew up he became head stockman for many years, as did his son, another John Mitchell who was head stockman on "Belltrees" for over twenty-five years. Now, George Mitchell and his family live in a cottage beside "The White Cottage" where his forebears lived one hundred and fifty years ago.

Cecil McInnes came to the district in 1921 with a mob of cattle from Gloucester and applied for a job as stockman with H. L. White. In 1923 he married Ethel Smith who came from England and helped in the "Belltrees" homestead. Ethel McInnes told me recently that "H. L." said she,

> ". . . was the only one who knew how to make toast; he liked it nice and thick, you see, and when he went and stayed at the Hotel Australia they made the toast so thin he would not put it in his mouth . . ."

Cecil and Ethel McInnes were married in the "Belltrees" Chapel and later two of their sons, Jim and Cecil Jnr., worked on the property. In the 1950's, Jim managed the White's property "Willalooka" in South Australia and later "Terreel" at Gloucester. Cecil's two daughters, Jeannie and Winnie, helped first "A. H.'s" wife, Judy Lorna, and then me for many years in our homes until they also got married in the Chapel. Ethel McInnes recalls that when Mr. and Mrs. A. H. White were first married, "A. H." brought his new bride to meet the McInnes family and as they were leaving Mrs. McInnes asked Mrs. White if she would like some fresh farm eggs. She said she would "That was fifty-three years ago," Ethel McInnes said recently, "and we have been supplying your family with eggs every week ever since." And so they have. Other relatives of Cecil McInnes have also worked on "Belltrees" — before him, Neil McInnes, a shepherd in the 1860s, and his brother Archie, a bullock driver. Another Archie McInnes, a nephew of the shepherd, was called "Bung" and he, his brother and Jim McGregor were legends around the local rodeo circuit, all brilliant horsemen with great balance and no fear. They accepted other than for a few periods when he suffered a couple of setbacks, Alec was to be in the saddle almost every day for the rest of his life. At only three, he was lighting pieces of stringy bark and his flannelette nightshirt caught fire. He had twenty-eight pieces of skin grafted to his left shoulder in a miraculous piece of surgery done by Sir Alexander MacCormack. Although this has meant his not being able to lift his left arm above his shoulder, it has not prevented Alec from carrying out all the tasks allotted to him.

Alec came to "Belltrees" in 1928 whilst droving for "Ellerston" where his father had been bookkeeper and storekeeper and his family had primary grants nearby. Alec is not only an institution on this property but an acknowledged great horseman, well-known throughout the Hunter Valley and the States of New South Wales and Queensland for his incredible campdrafting ability. In 1936, 1937, 1938 and 1940 Alec was selected in the New South Wales campdrafting team to challenge Queensland for the Australian championship. There were four men in each team and Alec rode his famous horse, Barry. It was at this time that New South Wales won three consecutive championships. In 1939, Alec was again selected to compete in the Police Boys' Carnival at the Sydney Showground, and for those who really understand campdrafting scores, Alec gained 93 points on each of his two runs taking the championship on Arrawidgee with 186 points — a magnificent score. Alec has bred and educated many well-known stock horses — Mopsy, Cooldust, Bimbimby, Sheba, Butcher and Beenabonnet amongst others. Alec has at least twenty-three championship ribbons as well as a trunk load full of trophies. His advice on campdrafting and his knowledge of stock horse breeding is still eagerly sought.

Alec Wiseman remains a refreshing reminder of the "old school". Whatever job came his way he did with a smile, never minding how long it took or at what hour of the day it was given to him. Alec's temperament and inherent general rural knowledge have contributed greatly to the development and improvement of the "Belltrees" cattle, sheep and horse herds. He always instructed used to say, and the stock would remain calm. "This is an art," said Alec. Prim still recalls today how much she relied on Alec. His interest and sympathetic understanding enabled her to get out of the house and onto the property that she so much enjoyed. And, "when Dad roared at me, Alec would take me to his home and give me sponge cake." It was typical of his marvellous disposition. In his quiet way, he capably carried out all "A. H.'s" directives and he has taught my husband, Michael, and my son, Antony, sound, basic knowledge of horse and stock management. Because Alec has kept them in contact with the past, he has helped provide the continuity that "Belltrees" has enjoyed for four generations.

Alec and Mrs. Wiseman have lived on "Belltrees" now for forty-eight years. Today Alec is a fund of yarns about the old days. "You see I can remember when there were no aeroplanes," he told me. "I can see the horses now at 'Ellerston' when the first plane went overhead. They galloped around in fright for an hour and a half until they were covered in lather. Now, when a plane flies over, they don't even lift their heads from their feed."

Men like Alec Wiseman have been the backbone not only of progress and prosperity on "Belltrees" but, indirectly, through their example, they have been the eternal rocks on which the foundations of rural Australia have been established.

Alec Wiseman also represents a living link between "Belltrees" and the neighbouring property of "Ellerston", which was sold by the White family in 1924. Alec Wiseman's great-grandfather, George Aslin, was the first manager for the White family on "Ellerston". In 1871, Henry Charles White, appointed George James Cobb, to assist him with the running of "Ellerston". George James Cobb was succeeded by his son, George F. Cobb for whom Alec Wiseman worked. Alec admired George F. Cobb tremendously. "He was a wonderful man with men," Alec recalls, "and made a lot of money for the Whites." George F. Cobb managed "Ellerston" for over twenty-five years, having been at "Belltrees" for ten years prior to that. His son, Hunter Cobb, carried on a long line of service by managing "Belltrees" for "A. H." when he went overseas in 1933.

Thomas Taylors moved to Liverpool but Frank preferred to stay. For George F. Cobb had looked after Frank since he was nine years old, giving him odd jobs polishing silverware and cleaning boots. By age eleven, Frank was a cowboy and a milkman and when he married Annie Pinkerton he teamed with his brothers-in-law to form Taylor and Pinkerton Brothers, who began to purchase land of their own. Frank died in 1979 at the age of ninety-six by which time the Taylor family had accumulated 15,000 acres of their own land in the Upper Hunter area. The dedication of this family to "Belltrees" in its formative years secures for them an important place in "Belltrees" history.

The Jarvis family first settled the "Wet Creek" area of "Belltrees". But like other families they gradually became absorbed into the "Belltrees" workforce. In the 1930s, a descendant of this original family, Fred Jarvis, did a magnificent job restoring the old slab store. His brother, Bill, was also a wonderful bushworker. He took over from his uncle Bill Dearman as bullock driver for "Belltrees" and once made twenty bullock yokes for his team with his own axe out of river oak.

Another great character of the times was Tom Cronin who lived nearby. He came to "Belltrees" in the late 1880s. He lived in the pear paddock, so named because large pits were dug there to bury prickly pear in tin boxes. The pear was so dense that before Tom and Mrs. Cronin could leave their hut near the pepper trees, they had to put a bullock hide over the neck of a draught horse and have it drag a log to clear a path enabling them to get out. Mrs. Cronin, it is said, used to ferment the prickly pear and make a quite pleasant alcohol.

It was Tom Cronin who built the first dam on "Belltrees" using only a horse and scoop. It took him two years. Today, a similar dam, built with a bulldozer would take two days. Tom Cronin is best remembered as the rouseabout in the shed at shearing time. He was a small, balding man with a big tobacco-stained moustache. He used to wear a thick, grey woollen

Aubrey Jarvis, a typical bush worker, fencing at Colonel's Swamp. March 1920. *H. L. White.*

Jim McGregor, an employee at "Belltrees" for 50 years.
Raking the church yard July, 1923.
H. L. White.

Harry McPhee and Cecil McInnes sitting on a wool basket.
Country Life.

Australian Light Horse.

Tom Weightman belonged to much the same period, though no one is certain where he came from, when he arrived or even how old he was. Tom just wouldn't tell and he had no relatives with whom these things could be checked. It's thought he was born around 1830 and he performed all manner of odd jobs on "Belltrees" from working in the shearing sheds to tendering the vegetable garden. Because he had no relatives when he died at approximately ninety years of age, a special plaque in the Chapel commemorates his service.

Another of "Belltrees" "institutions" was Alby Rose. Born about 1890, he came to "Belltrees" as a teenage cowboy, was head stockman in the period between John Mitchell and Alec Wiseman, and remained on "Belltrees", in all, for sixty-two years. Alby was meticulous in counting sheep. If "A. H." went away to buy a mob he would always take Alby with him. A story grew up about Alby that he used to carry in his saddle bag only enough tea and sugar for a quart pot full of tea. If he knocked that over, hot water was the alternative. The story concludes that Alby had the unbelievable record of not knocking the quart pot over once in sixty-two years.

The Eipper family was typical of many in the incidental rather than deliberate way in which they began their service at "Belltrees". Len Eipper's father died in 1896 leaving a wife and a son, Len, then only eleven. Len started to earn a living carting wood around Scone; then he bought a waggon and soon, with his horse-drawn waggon, was carting "Belltrees" wool. As he progressed, he had a bigger waggon made and his pride and joy was "Excelsior" made by W. T. Bennett of St. Mary's. On October 6, 1920, Len Eipper took a load of seventy bales of W. W. W. wool to Scone. "H. L." wanted to take a photo of the load but didn't believe that Len would make it through the river crossings. So "H. L." followed him and when he arrived in Scone took the photo.

Soon after Len's father died, his mother came to "Belltrees" to when our children Wendy and Scott were small it was Geoff's daughter Gwen who helped me at the "Farm".

There were other families too who set their roots in "Belltrees" during "H. L.'s" time. Ben Ellery started with "the boss" as a farmer working with a horse and plough. His three sons, Jack, Essie and Claude, succeeded him and were the first men on "Belltrees" to use tractors in the 1930s. During World War II they worked tirelessly to produce the extra wheat crops which were so urgently needed.

And there was Win Thrift, who came to "H. L." as his chauffeur. Wherever "H. L." went by car, Win Thrift drove him. In 1924, "H. L." opened the road from Scone to Barrington Tops and Win Thrift, with "H. L." aboard, was the first man to negotiate his way, in a car, to the top.

Thomas Moran gave fifty-two years of loyal and willing help to "Belltrees" and descendants of his live still today in Scone. Bob Leggett is another of "H. L.'s" employees whose name lives on. He was a farmer on "Belltrees" for over thirty-one years and his reputation still survives for digging perfectly straight furrows with his horse and plough. As I mentioned earlier, he brought great honour to "Belltrees" when his variety of maize, "Leggett's Pride", won an international award at Wembley, England. Bob Leggett's friend, Bob Hudson, was the blacksmith at the same time. He was a great tradesman. He is remembered for making all the hinges and gate fasteners on the wooden gates around the property, still a feature of the station. "A. H." designed the special "drop tongue" patent gate fastener and Bob Hudson made them in his forge.

At the same time, the Greer family lived across the River from the station. Jim and Bill were stockmen and boundary riders and a sister, Maude, who later lived in Gundy, used to come to "Belltrees" to do the laundry, uncomplainingly starching and ironing numerous white damask tablecloths and napkins. Jim's son, Freddie, became the station butcher while the daughters, Florence, Annie and Mary helped Judy Lorna White when she lived at "Kioto". In a continuation of their connection with would drive around in the AHW 222 utility truck doing numerous repair jobs together.

It is easy to see how loyalty and commitment grew out of involvement such as this — an involvement which for many "Belltrees" workers dated back half a century or more.

Two branches of the McPhee family have a special association. Each had a Duncan McPhee. The first of these families owned "Ferndale" and "Wyoming", adjacent to "Belltrees". Donald McPhee, the father, was a member of the "Belltrees" cricket team for forty years and at sixty-four was still wicketkeeper/captain. His son, Duncan, was a magnificent shearer and held the highest tally in the "Belltrees" shed. In 1970, Michael and I bought "Ferndale" and "Wyoming" together with the western flank of Mt. Woolooma.

It is, however, the other Duncan McPhee family, from "H. L.'s" time, that was more immediately involved with "Belltrees". This Duncan McPhee had five sons, Norman, Ron, Harry, Keith and Eric, all of whom were brilliant horsemen. Ron could teach a horse to do anything and legend has it that he also taught sheepdogs to obey orders in reverse just to tease the jackaroos. When they called "come behind" the dog would go up front and turn the mob. Harry McPhee spent all his life on "Belltrees" and "Terreel" except when he went away to World War II. During the War he was taken prisoner, worked on the Burma Road and was imprisoned in the dreaded Changi Prison Camp where he cared for his Lieutenant, Peter Playfair, and Henry Hordern. The families of both these men became involved in "Belltrees" through marriage, Henry Hordern being Michael's first cousin and Peter Playfair, the brother-in-law of Michael's sister, Morna. It was a fortuitous meeting but Harry virtually saved their lives. He was a thin but strong and tough bushman and he taught his two city counterparts how to keep alive under fearful conditions. But Harry McPhee was a shy, unassuming fellow never one to take credit. He contributed greatly to stock management on "Belltrees" and Michael says he was the most talented man he has ever worked with in the

Belltrees Stockmen on station stockhorses, 1953.
Tom McInnes, Bobby McInnes, Jim McInnes, Alec Wiseman, Cecil McInnes, Kevin Grant and Brian Hayes. *James Fitzpatrick.*

much quieter disposition, was also named Jim McGregor. When he became ill soon after he arrived at "Belltrees" in 1903, "H. L." sent him on a boat trip to Vancouver to recover. Jim McGregor never forgot this kind deed and when he retired he moved to Terrigal to look after Louisa Maude White. At the age of seventy-two he wrote her a letter expressing his pride that he had just learnt to read and write.

One family whose numerical strength alone has earned them a special place in "Belltrees" history is the Rossington family. They came from Yorkshire, England, and for many generations helped as blacksmiths on "Belltrees". George Rossington, the first to arrive, was a farmer who had eight children, one of whom was Isiah, known as "Ike". "Ike" set up as a blacksmith at Gundy and Moonan Flat. He used to shoe the horses at "Belltrees", making his way here by sulky once a month. He would often shoe seventeen horses, making all the shoes himself and return home to Gundy by 4 o'clock. "Ike" and his wife, Emily Jane, had sixteen children, including two sons, Aubrey and Lance, who also worked as blacksmiths. Aubrey inherited "Ike's" incredible memory for knowing the exact size of any shoe of any horse he had shod. Michael says that he could call into Aubrey's shop at Gundy and say, "The chestnut mare with the white blaze has thrown a shoe," and in the mail coach the next day, four shoes would arrive and fit the mare to perfection. Aubrey enlisted in World War II and became a farrier with the 12/24 Light Horse.

Of her sixteen children, Emily Rossington had five sons who served in the A.I.F. and she was very proud of her brooch with the five stars. Two younger sons, Alwyn and Jim also worked at "Belltrees" doing fencing and other general tasks alongside two of their cousins, Myrvine and Lloyd Rossington. All of them were strong, fit and capable workers.

But perhaps the son of "Ike" that we know best was Clifton Herbert Rossington, better known as "Tippo". "Tippo" was a stockman here for twenty years, the comic relief of the station always ready for a prank or a laugh. If you stopped to chat to

"Ike" Rossington 1947.
Kindly lent by Lance Rossington.

had to go to Sydney for treatment. In a brief history of the Rossington family which Lance wrote and forwarded to me, he incorporated this story:

> ". . . the Rossington family are indeed very grateful to Mr. A. H. White for his generous help and concern over Ike's illness. Ike was in Sydney when the doctors told him there was no more they could do for him. Mr. White sent a car down from Scone specially to bring him home. 'Take a week if you have to, but don't knock him about,' were Mr. White's instructions to the driver."[1]

"Tippo" married Betty Golledge, daughter of Maude Golledge (Maude Greer). "Tippo" was a marvellous father. He and Betty had seven children. There were always cars parked outside their cottage whilst they were at "Belltrees". I have never known such hospitable parents and such thoughtful children. Three of "Tippo's" daughters, Lyn, Marlene and Jenny helped me when our children were small, Lyn coming to me when Wendy was a baby, Marlene when I had Camilla and Jenny when Mark Jim was young. The three girls always displayed remarkable patience and understanding of small children and would play peacefully with them. Marlene was fifteen when she received her first wages from me. She smiled and said, "Now I can put a suit on lay-by for Dad." I have never experienced such unselfishness or concern for each member of the family as that branch of the Rossington family generated for one another. It was primarily because of this example that we decided to have seven children in the hope that our "seven little Australians" would be as considerate towards one another as were the children of the "Tippo" Rossington family.

Michael Francis White 1981. *Laurence Le Guay.*

and "Belltrees" Today

MICHAEL AND I were in Adelaide on March 6, 1964, when Morna rang to tell us that "A. H." had died suddenly from a heart attack in Sydney that morning. "A. H." had been unwell intermittently for several years and had spent much of his time in his flat in Sydney in semi-retirement. Yet his death was a great shock to the family. He was only sixty-three years of age. We flew back for the private funeral immediately, and I well remember driving to the crematorium with my mother-in-law, Judy Lorna White. "There will just be red roses on the coffin," she said, "there will be no card." I felt unbelievably sad for her, understanding as I did what the loss of this powerful man, her late husband, would mean to her life and to "Belltrees". Throughout his active working life there had been only one way to get along with "A. H." and that was to be subservient to him. Judy Lorna White and my husband knew this to be true. Yet, when the moment comes that the forceful decision-maker departs, a deep and irrevocable void remains.

Thankfully, mother and son possess the same patience and calm nature, an indefinable resolution in the face of adversity. Although Michael had managed "Belltrees" while his father had been ill, he was always conscious of a critical and analytical eye overseeing what he was doing. Now, for the first time, in March, 1964, Michael was on his own to take full responsibility of "Belltrees" and assume care for the interests of his mother and three sisters.

During this period, "Belltrees" was in a transitional phase. By from that known to his father. For during "A. H.'s" lifetime, he had given orders to at least nine stockmen every morning. At 7.30 a.m., these men waited near the office to receive their instructions from "the boss". This is the practice known as "line-up" which has persisted for over 100 years. Lateness was not brooked. But each boundary rider then had 3,000 acres of country to check, riding around the rabbit-proof fences six days a week to see that there were no holes or broken wires. But by 1970, "Belltrees" could not afford this, and Michael employed fewer men and personally rode the boundary on his Honda motorbike once a fortnight to check the fences. He then intensified every facet of production to produce fatter lambs, better horses and cattle and more crops on a smaller acreage. There were naturally increased problems under such a scheme but he adhered to the golden rule laid down by his forefathers of never over stocking your country if you wished to look after your land. This was part of the long term outlook, one of many policies based on the assumption of continuity of family ownership. Another emphasised the necessity of ridding the country of any spreading burrs; another was the importance placed on "the boss" being able to show an employee how to do any job, simply by being able to do it himself. The pursuit of these precepts has required each son to start at the bottom of the station ladder so that when his turn of management comes, he is able to scruff a calf, fence, lop trees, shoe a horse, plough, muster and sow crops as well as plan for future development. Over the desk in "A. H.'s" office he had pinned his motto:

> "The best fertilizer of any country is the footstep of the owner."

Michael lives by that today working alongside his fellow men. He takes his turn shovelling ensilage, fixing the station pump down the well and driving the bulldozer. Moreover, Michael believes that if a father hopes to perpetuate a dynasty, whether it be pastoral or professional, he must devote some of his own time to his children. And time is the universally scarce means. Much can be years jackarooing at "Brunette Downs", in the Northern Territory, and two trips overseas, he had spent eighteen years learning first hand the fundamentals of station life.

Michael and I became engaged in December, 1954 after I returned from England. We decided not to get married until I had completed my Economics degree and that gave us a year to build a new house. We had always admired the "cattle camp" site that great-uncle Arthur White selected for his home "Kioto", but the house itself was no longer able to be restored. The walls were badly cracked from the effect of extremes of wet and dry on the clay soil and bulls had been allowed to feed in the garden. We demolished "Kioto", cleaned all the mortar from the sandstock bricks and with the ingenious help and plans of the architect, John Suttor of Sydney, we built and transformed the old house into our new home, "Belltrees Farm". In 1955, whilst the farm was being built, a cyclone hit N.S.W. causing unprecedented floods to this area. Eighteen inches of rain fell in a fortnight and the Hunter River rose to a record level of 24 feet 6 inches at the station. Part of the only outlet road from our area was washed into the river leaving Gundy, Moonan Flat, "Belltrees" and "Ellerston" cut off from Scone. To overcome the emergency, "A. H." assumed leadership and created a goat track for through traffic. It was over this rather precipitous track that semi-trailers had to climb, loaded with all the building materials for our new house.

In February 1956, Michael and I were married and after our honeymoon we moved into our new Georgian Colonial home. Adjustment from an active city life to the quiet of the country was at first strange to me. Michael would take his sandwiches for lunch in his saddle bag and be gone for the day and somehow I had to fill in the interminable hours of the afternoon. My only companions were my black labrador pup "Keelo" and my palamino foal "Lani". Gradually, I attuned to life in the bush. Like any new bride, I worked hard at the interior decoration of our new home. I wanted to project my personality on to the surroundings and, more than anything, I wanted to create an atmosphere of welcome. One of the outstanding recollections of my childhood is of the fun, the sitting room smiling gently and I knew then that he thought the evening a success. Quietly, I said to myself "I've nearly captured the atmosphere I wanted and the White family enjoy it."

For twenty-five years now, "Belltrees Farm" has been the scene of many happy times. Our seven children, Antony, Peter, Wendy, Scott, Camilla, Mark and Edward have enjoyed children's parties and fancy dress parties. We have also had numerous dinner and dance evenings, Melbourne Cup lunches and even a circus on the lawn. At weekends, we have family picnics beside the Hunter River, walks to the waterfall in Woolooma gully or enjoy barbecues at our glass house retreat on the top of Mt. Woolooma. There is an ever-present communion with nature and a regular communication with our friends who call and stay at "Belltrees".

Michael, like his other forebears on "Belltrees", has always been interested in judging cattle. Since he was a small boy, he has worked in the stockyard whilst the cattle are being culled and through this practical experience has been able to develop an acute capacity for accurate appraisal of the quality of different types of animals. This ability has been widely recognised and he has judged in country shows and at Royal shows in all Australian capital cities. One of his most significant accolades was being invited to judge the Aberdeen Angus bulls at the Perth show and sales in Scotland in 1958. This was a tremendous honour as he was then only 29 years of age — the youngest man to be so invited. Soon after Christmas, 1957, we left "Belltrees" where the temperature had been 116 degrees in the "Belltrees Farm" dining room, and by the following weekend, we had arrived in Scotland amid sleet and snow.

I remember the judging day well. The morning of the show dawned cold and icy. We were ready in the vestibule at the Station Hotel in Perth at the appointed hour waiting to be collected by the Secretary of the Aberdeen Angus Society who had been delegated to escort the "judge" to the arena. The Secretary was newly married and we waited in the hallway for twenty minutes for his wife who had been undecided as to what warm hat she should wear. When she eventually appeared she thought she calmed both

Angus cattle and stockmen on "Belltrees". *James Fitzpatrick.*

sashing time. Neon lights had been installed but only at one end of the arena. The far end was plunged into darkness. The ring was the size of a tennis court with pillars down the centre and T.V. cameras and crews stationed between each pillar. The first event was for aged bulls and over sixty waddled in to be judged in prime condition. The judging ring became totally congested; the bulls crowded in to one another with the head of one overlapping the hind quarters of another in front. My heart was pounding. I had only watched Michael judging in Australia on grass lawns in daylight and with plenty of room. This was a nightmare. After the settling-in process of the first few classes, Michael gained confidence and judged with assurance. I could follow the type of bull he was after as he searched for size and scale. But to the Scotsman, where pedigree takes pride of place, Michael's judging was unconventional. He was sending the "bluebloods" from the arena as they were small, squat, pony-types, bred for the Argentine market while the larger confirmation bulls from unknown studs were receiving the awards and ribbons. I was not aware of the unpopular things he was doing until I read the evening papers: "Judge from down under turns tables upside down." The following day the sales were held and a bull that Michael had sent from the ring unplaced made the top price. Afterwards we received an urgent message from the BBC in London. They wanted us to go to the Glasgow T.V. studio and appear on Cliff Mitchelmore's "Tonight" programme. I dreaded the prospect for I knew that this programme was watched by eight million people throughout Britain and that Mr. Mitchelmore's success depended almost exclusively on creating controversy. Michael actually looked forward to the challenge and handled his interview very well. "If I judged those bull classes again, I would abide by the decision I made and again remove all dwarf-type bulls from the ring."

It was then my turn to be interviewed. Mitchelmore treated me as a little colonial girl and asked me about my life in the outback and the "sticks". I tried so hard to present a pleasant picture of our new little home, "Belltrees Farm", 13,000 miles away. Twelve champion, "Elegance of Charter House" had won international acclaim. It had been bought by Donald Grant in New Zealand in 1958 and later bought by an American syndicate in the U.S.A. What Michael had learnt in the stockyards at "Belltrees" with the constant handling and culling of Angus bulls had stood him in good stead.

During the same period in 1958, Michael was President of the Aberdeen Angus Society of Australia when sweeping changes were effected. Under his Presidency, not only did the name and constitution of the Society change but also our weddedness to the Scottish breed though the name Aberdeen Angus was removed and the breed in Australia became known as Angus. Also the domination of the Society by N.S.W. was broken down, a move of great importance to the breeding of Angus cattle in the Southern states. In March, 1969, the first international Angus forum was held at the Wentworth Hotel in Sydney. Michael was invited to be one of the nine speakers on a topic "The Management of Commercial Angus Herds." The theme of his address was the necessity to cull herds strictly and remove any inferior types of cattle. He spoke simply and practically in contrast to other more theoretical, academic speakers and many members of the forum later complimented him on his helpful advice.

At "Belltrees" it is always "the boss's" job to select the best bulls and cows and cull the ones lacking quality. This is a job that can never be delegated for if the standard of the cattle slips there is only "the boss" to blame. It is worth recalling that it is not only the "Belltrees" Whites who have honed a skill in breeding and judging stock. The same can be said today for Reg White of Timor; David and Dennis White of "Havilah", Mudgee; and Richard and Graham White of "Bald Blair", Guyra, New England.

Since droughts today have become a more recurring enemy of the pastoralist, it is never possible to assess the extent or consequences of severe seasonal conditions. Quite simply, the grazier must learn to prepare for disaster. In 1965, Michael was forced to sell 900 head of cattle in Geelong, Victoria. For the stock that were left at home, he had to open up ensilage pits and feed

Antony White feeds his working dogs.
Caroline Ryrie.

Camilla White tries out the horse and trap used in the Disney film "To ride a wild pony", 1974. *John Brothers and Associates.*

Mark Jim White, 1981 T.K.S.
John Bradshaw.

Wendy White passes her brother Peter, another polo stick during a polo practice. *Caroline Ryrie.*

today is being saved by 4,000 tonnes of conserved silage.

Drought times have also made the station manager aware of the value of water conservation. After the 1965 drought, Michael set aside an annual expenditure towards dam construction and with his own and other bulldozers constructed the Lapstone paddock dam in 1970, which now holds an estimated 35 million gallons of water giving cattle, in dry times, drinking water away from the river paddocks. This is essential because today, "Belltrees" is geared to a breeding and fattening cattle operation whereby 2,000 head of vealers, or light steers, are turned off in fat condition each year. The billiard room at the homestead is bedecked with ribbons won by "Belltrees" cattle in numerous fat stock show competitions.

With an eye on the future, but still respectful of the traditions of the past, Michael has never been afraid to diversify. When the Japanese meat trade in 1970 demanded early maturing and succulent carcasses, Charolais blood was infused into the "Belltrees" Angus cattle to produce Angus-Charolais crossed cattle, more suited to feed lots and the Japanese markets. But pastoral fortunes can never be anticipated. By 1974, world oil shortages had caused a slump in Japanese trade and a decline in the demand for this type of Australian beef. "Belltrees" suffered in the short term but we did prove that tender, marbled beef could be produced economically in Australia to meet the special requirements of Tokyo restaurants.

1970 produced other setbacks and drought struck again. Ten double-decker semi-trailers left "Belltrees" for Victoria where 759 head had to be sold. After this adverse season, heavy summer rains fell in 1971 and the blowfly problem became insurmountable. Any amounts of diazanon had litle effect. Sheep died everywhere and Michael decided to disperse the whole flock.

By September, 1976 my mother-in-law, Judy Lorna White, had spent fifty years of her life at "Belltrees" homestead and we decided to hold a family dinner in her honour. About this time, she realised that the upkeep of the big house was becoming too much for her to manage. When she was not taking advantage of the mother had been an excellent housekeeper and every vestige of White memorabilia had been meticulously kept. Therefore, the transition was easy. I just had to redecorate where it was needed. Firstly, the brown hall carpet runner needed renewing. It interested me that when I pulled it up, the section from the front door to the foot of the stairs was in perfect order while the section from the foot of the stairs to the dining room and the sitting room was threadbare. The carpet told its own story. For three generations, the homestead had been essentially a White family home, well used by members of the family but seldom used by guests from the front door.

My initial problem was how to introduce more light into the homestead as a means of creating an atmosphere of life. To keep out the heat and glare, generations of White women had all had the glass panes above the doorways coated with layers of cream paint. I mounted a ladder and, balancing a tin of stripper, scraped away the cream paint allowing more daylight to filter into the hall.

Altering a family home can be an emotional thing. There is always a certain loyalty to childhood reminiscences. But my object was to make welcome all members of the family and their friends. For the homestead has so much to offer with its history and heritage that it deserves to be shared with others. And in that sharing, I believe, a new and rewarding understanding emerges — an understanding of the sentimental value of memorabilia — of "H. L.'s" surveyor's chain; of his boyhood egg collection; of Aunt Millie's painting and her Japanese teapot in a padded basket; of Judy Lorna White's sewing basket; of "A. H.'s" series of colt pistol photos; of Dorothy Minell's doll's house made from old boxes by Jim McGregor; of Michael's *Boys' Own Annuals*; and the childhood photo in the smoke room of Louisa Maude with ringlets and pink cheeks. At Christmas 1980, Judy Lorna White, her four children, four in-laws, nineteen grandchildren and one great-grandchild stayed and celebrated Christmas in the "Belltrees" homestead. Each member of the family knows that this will always remain the

The Michael White family set off on horses for a picnic. 1971. *Sheena Gilmour.*

Top: The Belltrees homestead at night. *Laurence Le Guay.*
Above Left: The sitting room, introducing light. *Laurence Le Guay.*
Above Right: The dining room at "Belltrees Farm", using the same dining table as Mr. & Mrs. Arthur White used at "Kioto", one hundred years previously (see p. 102). *Max Easton.*

Top Left: The Playfair family join us in a walk to the waterfall in Woolooma Gully. *M. F. White.*
Top Right: "Belltrees Farm". The gum tree in the foreground was planted by Arthur White 90 years ago. He bought the seedling home in his saddle bag. *Laurence Le Guay.*
Above: Edward White reads the lesson in the family chapel. The Rev. Ernest Bailey looks on. *M. F. White.*

Above: Michael White feeds ensilage to the Angus bulls during the 1980 drought. *Laurence Le Guay.*

Left: Lamb tailing takes place during the school holidays, the children love to help the men. *M. F. White.*

family seat of the "Belltrees" Whites and it is here to celebrate any event which brings the family together.

Over the years we have enjoyed playing country host to many well-known people. In 1970, Her Royal Highness, Crown Princess Sonja of Norway came to stay. In the same year, His Excellency, Sir Paul Hasluck, Governor-General of Australia, visited. We have welcomed Lord Snowdon whose step-mother Carol was Judy Lorna White's sister. In 1979, Their Royal Highnesses the Duke and Duchess of Gloucester, and their two children, stayed at "Belltrees". Other guests have included Their Excellencies, the Governor-General of Australia, Sir Zelman Cowen and Lady Cowen; General Sir Maurice Dowse from London, who has spent two family Christmases with us; and many friends from England, France and Norway especially Agnes and Niels Werring. Of course, the greatest honour of all was the visit of His Royal Highness, Prince Charles, The Prince of Wales, who came to play polo and stayed overnight at "Belltrees" in October, 1974.

What I hope this suggests is that, today, the homestead is being used. The children each have their own room and in school holidays invite many friends to stay. Music blares and the dust in the billiard room is never allowed to settle. Gradually the Victorian way of life that the homestead enjoyed in the old days is undergoing transformation. Who would have imagined then that the homestead would provide the setting for two films — the Walt Disney production "Ride a Wild Pony" in 1974 and the ABC production "She'll Be Sweet" starring Sally Kellerman and Tony Lobianco in 1977. While the homestead is not open to the general public, the National Trust has made two visits and we have permitted a group from the Art Gallery Society of N.S.W., under the guidance of my friend Ann Lewis, to visit "Belltrees". The Elizabethan Theatre Trust and other interested women's groups have also been allowed to come but only when under the expert and tutored eye of Shirley Hay.

While changes have occurred within the homestead, the centre piece of "Belltrees", changes are inevitable outside. Michael's keen interest in horse sports means that "Belltrees" is used for various horse activities. In January each year, Majorie Holloway, of Aberdeen, holds a pony camp here on the sportsground. Twenty-eight children stay in the shearing huts and are educated in how to train and handle their ponies. The camp lasts ten days and many city children are, in this way, given exposure to rural Australia along with the opportunity to ride their ponies and improve their riding skills. Every February, a

Above: The Scone polo club lines up for the "Wootton cup" 1972 on the Belltrees polo ground.

Gymkhana is held on the "Belltrees" sportsground to raise funds for the Church of England. All the women from the various parishes help with lunch and stalls, whilst the husbands organise the horse sports. It's not unusual to see the quietest children's pony laden with an entire, smiling family until the pony signals enough; or tiny tots' noses sometimes barely visible under velvet riding hats.

The polo season makes "Belltrees" a special focus for polo enthusiasts. In 1970, the Scone polo club had to vacate the "Yarrandi" ground and Michael made two polo grounds on "Belltrees" as an alternate site. These are now officially used by the Scone polo club and lie on the original "Broomfield" grant of 1831. There are approximately thirty-two playing polo members in Scone and practices and matches are held throughout the season. Each weekend, family and friends meet for picnic lunches and watch the men play. By July, the club holds its own polo carnival and teams come from as far as Queensland, South Australia, Victoria and numerous parts of N.S.W. to compete. In 1972, an Argentine team played an Australian team on the "Belltrees" ground before a crowd of 3,000. When his Royal Highness, Prince Charles, played on the ground in 1974 it was in October, rather late for our polo season. But many players, Angus Munro, Jaime Mackay, Hugh Higgins, Rod Murchison, Rob Vickery, Ted

Above: Memo Gracida, U.S.A. enjoys a practice game at "Belltrees" before competing at the R.A.S. show, 1981. *Caroline Ryrie.*

Right: H.R.H. Prince Charles discussing the polo game with Michael White between chukkas. October, 1974. *John Fairfax & Sons.*

Edwards and James Archibald kept their horses in training for the event. Threatening clouds hung in the sky all day but fortunately the deluge only broke after Prince Charles had hit the winning goal for his team. After the game, when the rain had abated, Michael invited Prince Charles to ride over the hills back to the "Belltrees" homestead. For six miles they enjoyed the freedom of riding a good horse over hilly terrain, occasionally chasing kangaroos that crossed their path. The Prince of Wales was most impressed with the Australian oilskin coat lent to him for the ride.

In 1979, a "one-day event" equestrian course was constructed across the river from the polo ground. Twenty-four jumps were built utilising the river, the river flats, hills and gullies. Nicola Cramsie from Ireland and Dordie Bragg planned the course; while Michael, Arthur Bragg and other willing helpers constructed the solid jumps. There are stone walls, steps, slides into the Isis river and sky jumps — all destined to test equestrian skills. Each September a "One-Day Event" is held on the course and last year there were eighty competitors. In 1979, the event was won by the Olympian, Wayne Roycroft.

So the Hunter Valley is often rightly regarded as the home of horsemanship. Our eldest son, Antony, competes in local rodeos and has scored high points in campdrafting events riding his two horses Annabelle and Trumby. The "firm" of H. E. A. & V. White continues to concentrate on breeding good stock horses and since Michael, Antony, Peter and Scott enjoy their polo, it is necessary to breed fast, safe polo ponies for the future.

Ten years ago, Brenda Ogilvie came from New Zealand to Australia seeking experience on an Australian cattle station. She joined us at "Belltrees" for three months after the Royal Easter Show and then went on to Queensland. When she returned before Christmas in that year, Michael invited her to stay on to prepare thirteen polo horses for the proposed visit to Australia, the following Easter, by an Argentine polo team. Since then, Brenda has filled many roles at "Belltrees". She has assisted me greatly in the demanding task of running such a large and busy household. But her native love of the outdoors and her skill with, and understanding of animals have also been invaluable in the day to day "Belltrees" activities.

Now, in 1981, "Belltrees" is experiencing the worst drought in living memory. Our average rainfall is normally 26 inches yet in the last eighteen months "Belltrees" recorded rainfall has been less than 17 inches. The consequences of such a drought on farmers in the Hunter Valley may well be felt for many years to come. Yet I marvel at Michael's optimism. Already we have sent thirty-five

Antony White competes in campdrafting events at Bushmen's carnivals throughout the Hunter Valley.

double-decker semi-trailers of cattle to Victoria and 900 head of cattle were sold in Colac last March. John Richardson of H. F. Richardson & Co., Geelong, Victoria has helped the "firm" through three droughts in 1965, 1970 and 1980; and the co-operation of his organisation has, in reality, saved part of our Angus herd. I suppose Michael's optimism derives from the belief that it is easier today than it was in olden days to limit the effects of drought. For example, he has been able to transport cattle to greener country whereas previously they had to walk along stock routes where there was neither water nor feed. He has opened up ensilage pits and effected the building of dams which have facilitated the use of paddocks where no natural water is left.

But the seasons are changing and the incidence of drought and its effect on all Australians may challenge the national will in the future more than they have at any time in the past. There has been, at best, only limited relief from this drought but it is pleasing to see father and son, Michael and Antony, working alongside each other, experience and youth together in a united determination to keep "Belltrees" on the move. Each day all decisions and cattle movements are recorded in the station diary not just as a record but also as a guideline for future generations when their moment of decision making comes. Consultation of past station records and a comparison with other drought years have helped in present times. They generate the spirit that "if they were able to pull through in the old days we can do likewise today."

Respect for one's heritage and the responsible acceptance of a legacy mean many things. Not only do they mean the passing on of records, stock, land and buildings; but more importantly they embody a challenge to see that a typically Australian way of life is understood, maintained and improved. The modern democratic tax structure and the need for smaller acreages have prevented vast profits being made that can be expended on the preservation of the historic buildings of "Belltrees", as happened in the past. The White family have refused any assistance from public trust sponsorship as this would mean the sacrifice of privacy and independence. Michael is forever vigilant in his responsibility to the "Belltrees" heritage and has tried to maintain the old buildings. "The White Cottage" of 1832, the part of the original homestead of around 1836 and the slab store of the same period are all in good condition. But it sometimes worries Michael that he may be blamed for not spending enough money on other old buildings. In 1969, he sold extra cattle for the purpose of cleaning and painting "The White Cottage" and the original homestead block in order to preserve the sandstock bricks. He repaired the roofs on the old stables, the old hay shed and the shearing shed. These are massive roof areas involving huge costs especially when buildings such as the great Horbury Hunt masterpiece, the shearing shed, have almost outlived their practical use. But the demand for capital expenditure is constant. Some guttering and outside woodwork on the homestead are rotten and need replacing, a mammoth undertaking. The wooden framework of the shearing shed needs attention and the lead in the stained glass windows of the family chapel is buckling. It is perhaps difficult for younger generations to understand that spending money on the preservation of old buildings is important. The values of the young are often more practical, more short term, more "here and now" — and, who knows, possibly more correct. But at a time when all Australians are growing more conscious of their past, I believe that every effort must be spent to preserve aspects of that past.

Our eldest son, Antony, left The King's School, Parramatta, six years ago and has worked on "Belltrees" for the last four years. He is full of enthusiasm and vigor. He treats the present drought as a great experience, even if he admits to being rather glad that it happened when he "had Dad here or I would not have been able to handle it." He says he has learnt much from his father and Alec Wiseman,

> "but I am young and I have new ideas and it is just hard to put them into practice. I'd like to really get "Belltrees" ticking — devote more time to other people's leisure time. I'd have horse schools, trail riding, utilise the place in every way. It's hard to know what the other members of the family want to do yet but the place has to be worked as a unit. If we divided it into 2,000 acre blocks, one could not make a living out of it . . ."

Antony praises his forebears for what they have done but fears,

> "that "Belltrees" may be known for what it was yesterday rather than for what it is today, and that is sad . . . I hope people don't look upon "Belltrees" as buildings. I like them to look around outside too. We could never start and create "Belltrees" from scratch like the past generations did. I admire all they have done, but now *we* must achieve something, it's just not good enough to mark time . . ."

Fortunately, Antony possesses the energy, the commitment and the will to fulfil these ambitions.

All these qualities have already been tested by the various demands of boarding school life. Our children have enjoyed some success at school but it is a mistake to think that any achievement at school, or in life, can come easily. In 1973, Antony was a member of the touring King's School Rugby Football Team and captained the side in the centenary match against The King's School, Canterbury in England. Subsequently he represented T.K.S. in rugby, cricket and track and field; captained the combined G.P.S. First Fifteen in 1974; played first grade rugby for Randwick and represented N.S.W. Country against Wales in 1978.

Anto's other brothers, Peter and Scott, also played for The King's School's First Rugby Fifteen and Peter won several G.P.S. hurdle and sprint championships. Wendy captained Frensham, Mittagong at cricket and both she and Camilla have represented their school in other activities. A younger brother, Mark, won a G.P.S. hurdles event in 1980 while Edward, "Edward the seventh", has just begun at Tudor House.

It pleases both Michael and me that the children show an athletic interest and a willingness to pursue goals and accept challenge, because positive attitudes to rural life will be needed and tested in the future. The sixth generation to run "Belltrees" will require a new framework of management just as Michael did in March, 1964. Today, the Hunter Valley is undergoing drastic changes. Open-cut coal mining, the construction of power stations and the building of aluminium smelters are transforming the quiet rural life of the district. Graziers will be forced to compete for labour and wages with industries developing on their doorstep. Land values and rates will rise in proportion to the competitive demand for the land and to the growing need for factory sites and residential areas.

But land owners have been challenged before. In overcoming the challenges today they have the added advantage of possessing a first hand knowledge of the country they love and understand. Granted a fall of rain, I am confident they will continue to enjoy a way of life, proudly independent and enviably Australian.

Conclusion

IT IS NOW MARCH, 1981 and once again I am in our retreat at the top of Mt. Woolooma. Some rain has fallen on "Belltrees", but I realise that only partial relief has been given from this harrowing drought. Nonetheless, as the fog lifts, I can see that some of the former beauty of this area has returned.

I am now aware that my journey into the past is almost over. Through it, I have seen "Belltrees" in all its personal and natural hues. I have marvelled at what has been achieved and the benefits that six generations of one Australian family have brought to this one small part of Australia.

In the pioneer, James White, one sees a conscientious man, devoted to his stock, his land and the improvement of both. His second son, Francis, though no less concerned with these, was a kindly and public spirited man who gave much of his time in the community's cause. The bulwark of the next generation, "H. L.", brought to the meticulous execution of what he did a brilliance born of tenacity, consolidating the pastoral achievements of his uncles, James and Henry Charles, but adding to them an understated sense of nationalism.

But, along the arc created by the pendulum of White history at "Belltrees", "A. H." reveals a greater affinity with the character and approach of the early pioneer James. "A. H." resented the time and the finance his father had spent on hobbies and interests outside the realm of "Belltrees". To him, "Belltrees" was the goal and he became fanatical about every detail on the property. For "H. L.", perfection seemed to be a state in which Australia was pulling together in harmonious achievement. For "A. H.", perfection was "Belltrees" at its best.

Michael could not help but be conscious of the standard set by his father. But he has wanted "Belltrees" to be part of a district and a community rather than an isolated world of its own. He became a member of the Scone Shire Council, the board of the Scott Memorial Hospital and the Agricultural Advisory Panel of the farm of Dr. Barnardo's Homes in Scone. He is Chairman of the Advisory Council of Tocal Agricultural College at Paterson; Chairman of Pitt Son and Badgery and an elected Councillor of the Royal Agricultural Society of N.S.W. Inheriting his grandfather's love of bird life, he has noted one hundred and sixty-four different species of birds around the "Belltrees" homestead for the R.A.O.U. Atlas of Australian Birds. He has done all this while maintaining an awareness of the "Belltrees" heritage and a commitment to its preservation.

Yet with Antony there is a striking resemblance to his grandfather, "A. H.", through his belief that voluntary work cuts deeply into one's time. At such a young age, he has devoted all his working hours to "Belltrees" alone. But in spite of the differences in attitudes and approach, a deep sense of pride and duty unites all generations of Whites on "Belltrees". And these qualities, I believe, provide a link between this family and all Australians whose sense of pride and duty has taken our country successfully in many directions. For the six generations at "Belltrees", it has meant a determination to maintain and improve this pastoral holding. To those who have spent all their lives here, whether it be for eight decades or one, "Belltrees" is not a spectacular asset but a sentimental possession.

Many times in the past, it would have been more profitable for the White family to sell "Belltrees" and reinvest the proceeds of the property in other facets of Australian economic development. But each generation has maintained a steadfast commitment to values which transcend pecuniary gain. These values, in action, seek the preservation of this heritage of stock, buildings and beauty which so identify "Belltrees". Today, it is easy to bring up the next generation of White children in this atmosphere. They are able to enjoy the natural, carefree way of life; to create their own entertainment and, as a family team, to help in station life.

In 1981, the Hunter River Valley is undergoing great change. The rich alluvial flats along the river's course are the very lands that harbour vast quantities of valuable minerals, especially coal. Because this land is so agriculturally productive, it was naturally the first land to be taken up by primary grants in the early 19th century. As proof of the affinity that Hunter Valley pioneers developed with the land that they settled, there are numerous families in the Valley today who, for many generations, have occupied a place in the history of this area. The Whites of "Belltrees" are only one such family.

However, everybody knows that individuals and families are incidental to the path of progress. Now, today, governmental planning in this area has gathered momentum. Rapid change and the threatened dislocation of established ways, now loom large over the Hunter Valley. Already coal trucks dominate the main arterial roads of the Valley and feasibility studies are trying to convince vignerons that "fallout" from aluminium smelters will not affect their grapes or wine. Many landowners face a future of uncertainty. They do not know, whether or not, their properties are to be resumed for open-cut mining. It is impossible not to be concerned by these developments especially when I reflect on the peaceful surroundings in which my writing has taken place.

In these surroundings, I have tried to open a window for the reader onto "Belltrees" history and in seeking to do this I have been, as it were, all the time in the room, surrounded by that history — by volumes of letters, books, catalogues, diaries, albums, photos and memorabilia. All this has intensified my feeling of belonging. We would hate to be told to leave this historic site.

When I first came from Sydney to "Belltrees", I found it difficult to understand the deep attachment that every member of the White family held for it. In every decision that was made, whether it was managerial, financial, developmental, ecological or personal, the property "Belltrees" came first. Now, twenty-five years later, I feel the same way. It is this strong feeling that has driven me on, often unconsciously, to unfold the story of "Belltrees".

Appendix

Appendix 1 – CHAPTER THREE

Diary of James White (MSS 1008)
"Journal of Occurances on board the ship 'Fairfield' from Cowes to New South Wales 12th March, 1826.

The Author was entrusted with 79 French Merino sheep belonging to the A.A. Co. The journal is the record of the sheeps' behaviour and ailments aboard. Some extracts . . .

March 12, 1826. Took on board the Fairfield at Cowes 79 Merino sheep.

March 13. All sheep sick. 25 very lame with footrot (The shepherds Richard Marchant and William May were also sick and unable to tend sheep).

March 16. One French Merino ewe died. Opened it up and found entrails injured. 24 very lame.

March 17. Sheep feed well and begin to take their water better. I have not given them more than 1 quart per day as I shall want more for them as the weather gets warm.

March 28. I have begun to shear some of those below as the weather is now very warm (Scab breaking out).

April 10. Two sheep above deck died. The heat overpowers those that are weak as it is still calm.

April 20. We have now just crossed the line with a fine breeze and I hope those sheep that are weak will soon be better.
(The sheep eat corn and hay). Merchant has a bad wound on his arm but is under the Captain's care).

May 11. The sea very rough. Sheep sick as Hatchway shut.

June 2. Sheep below are very well. Those on deck as usual. It came on about 1 o'clock at night. A most tremendous rough sea. One of the sheep pens on deck was in great danger of being washed overboard. They were filled with water several times during the night. The sheep on deck were very much injured particularly one that was very weak which I removed below directly but could not the others as the space below the main Hatchway was filled with sails. One of the pens below deck was removed with the dashing of the vessel and killed one of the sheep it was one which has been lame from the first taking them on board but had been for some time improving.

June 24. That sheep that was weak on deck died today. We came in sight of land.

June 25. I have used all the bran but as we have today got into the River Derwent hope we shall soon be able to get some at Hobart Town.

June 28. I have been to the Government Mills and bought some bran.

July 5. I have 50 which I am happy to say are in excellent condition.

July 18. Left the Harbour in Hobart Town.

July 19. Sea very rough. All the sheep very sick.

July 25. Landed 57 sheep at Sydney. Arr. Port Jackson.

August 1. Put 77 fleeces of wool into the stores."

Appendix 2 – CHAPTER FOUR

Yearly Wages and Names of Employees on "Belltrees" 12th February, 1888

Name	*Occupation*	*Wages Pds.*
Baker: John	Boundary Rider	55/-/-
Baker: Henry	Boundary Rider	50/-/-
Baker: Mary	House Servant (Ellerston)	26/-/-
Blenman: G.	Sheep Musterer etc.	65/-/-
Blenman: Wife	Men's Cook	
Bridge: Jas	Boundary Rider	40/-/-
Cobb: G. J.	Late Manager	500/-/-
Cobb: G. F.	Supt. Ellerston	200/-/-
Collins: Jas	Boundary Rider	50/-/-
Edwards: W.	Groom Gardener etc.	85/-/-
Edwards: Wife	Cook Belltrees	
Fogarty: A	Boundary Rider	50/-/-
Graham: R.	Store Keeper	100/-/-
Greer: Jas	Boundary Rider	50/-/-
Greer: Tos.	Boundary Rider	50/-/-
Hartney: Jno. Sr.	Sheep Overseer	62/-/-
Hartney: Jr.	Sheep mustering and burr cutting	32/10/-
Hawkins: Hy	Blacksmith and carpenter	88/8/-
Hodges: C.	Bullock driver	40/-/-
Jackson: Wm.	Sheep Mustering etc.	60/-/-
Kershaw: S.	Boundary Rider	65/-/-
Jackson: Jas	Sheep Mustering etc.	20/16/-
Kiley: Wm.	Boundary Rider	50/-/-
Lomax: Z	Burr Cutting etc.	35/-/-
McGregor: Jas	Sheep Droving, Building etc.	52/-/-
Mitchell: Geo	Stockman	60/-/-
Mitchell: Jno	Stockman	32/10/-
Roe: Joseph	Stockman	80/-/-
Roe: E.	Stockman	32/10/-
Roe: Wm.	Boundary Rider	50/-/-
Standford: W. O.	Storekeeper Ellerston	60/-/-
Taylor: Chas.	Boundary Rider	50/-/-
Taylor: Henry	Boundary Rider	50/-/-
Taylor: Thos.	Bullock Driver etc. Ellerston	65/-/-
Scriven: Wm.	Butcher	52/-/-
Tilse: F.	Boundary Rider	50/-/-
Vine: Jas	Boundary Rider	50/-/-
Watters: Chas.	Boundary Rider	50/-/-
Wood: Jno.	Boundary Rider	60/-/-
Willis: Geo.	Stockman & Drover etc.	40/-/-
Willis: Jno.	Sheep Mustering etc.	52/-/-
Willis Jno. jr.	Sheep Mustering etc.	2/10/-
White: H.L.	Supt.	250/-/-
	Total	2945/4/-

Appendix 3 – CHAPTER SIX

Notes on the H. L. White Collections

As shown elsewhere in this book H. L. White's interest in birds began in boyhood when he first collected eggs. He was later to become a member and staunch supporter of the R.A.O.U. (Royal Australian Ornithologists' Union) and an outstanding benefactor in ornithology. Inspired by the work of pioneer collectors such as A. J. Campbell at a time when vast areas of Australia were still unknown ornithologically, he employed field collectors to collect both bird-skins and eggs in remote regions of the country. He also carried out extensive purchase and exchange of material as part of a grand concept to form ornithological collections of national significance. From earliest times natural history has benefited from the liberality of devotees who have been in a position to foster its pursuit and H. L. White was a splendid Australian example of this generous ideal.

White chose well in the collectors he selected, e.g. Barnard, MacLennan, Jackson, Whitlock and others, of whom some spent many months at a time under rough conditions in the field and published accounts of their expeditions in *The Emu*. These accounts were not only eagerly awaited and read by Members of the R.A.O.U. at the time, but have remained most valuable records of the bird-life of the periods and regions concerned. A major significance of the H. L. White Collections lies in the fact that they were not only pioneering Collections, drawing together widely collected material, but also in that they have remained fundamental sources of data for ornithological research.

H. L. White's affection for the R.A.O.U. reflected in his financial Trust established for that organisation, and his contributions towards coloured plates in *The Emu*, was also shown in his desire that "collection(s) shall go to some institution where . . . members of the Union in question (R.A.O.U.) may have the advantage of examination for reference purposes, during other than business hours". Accordingly the conditions governing the donation of the Collection of bird-skins, received by the Museum in 1917, provided special access for Members of the R.A.O.U. between the hours of 7.30 p.m. and 10 p.m. on one evening each month. This was for a period of ten years and one can imagine that it must have provided a much appreciated opportunity for the serious students of the day in Melbourne and for visitors from the country or interstate, to examine an outstanding Collection.

The bird-skin Collection is particularly rich in central and northern Australian forms and although it is now not the only comprehensive source of such series, no research collection can be duplicated and the H. L. White Collection of bird-skins, as already mentioned, retains its scientific value as a source of data relating to particular species at particular places and times.

At the time of the presentation of the bird-skin Collection to the National Museum of Victoria (1917) both reference books and specimens from the inland and the north were few. The H. L. White Collection provided the field worker with magnificent reference material and, in fact, lessened the need for specimens to be sent overseas for determination. This significance applied equally to the Egg Collection, received by the Museum in 1927 following H. L. White's death.

The Egg Collection continues to be a remarkable source of information covering breeding distribution and habit. Both the Bird-skin and the Egg Collections have, for example, recently provided valuable data for the R.A.O.U. Atlas of Australian Birds, and the Land Conservation Council of Victoria's survey of Victorian regions in connexion with land use. Additionally, and over many years, they have provided data for a great many research workers throughout Australia and overseas.

H. L. White Collection of Bird-skins

Housed in ten black wooden cabinets separate from the remainder of the Museum's skin Collection, the H. L. White Collection contains over 8,500 specimens of almost entirely Australian species. Exceptions include three or four specimens from Lord Howe and Norfolk Island, a hawk from India, an Albatross from Japan and a plover from Egypt. The number of specimens entered in the register is 8,547. Of these some very few are nests, and three skins were sent to U.S.A. on donation and/or exchange in 1924.

The skins generally are in very good condition and are extremely well-prepared, and, while not carrying the very full data considered ideal today, consistently provide on their attached labels a distinctly higher level of information than most other collected specimens of the same period, including many in the National Museum Collection. The Collection is accompanied by a Register containing the registration of the specimens under number, date of registration, species name, sex, date of receipt and locality, to which has recently been added the name of the collector and date of collection. Additionally, there is a complete card catalogue of the Collection arranged alphabetically under species showing on a separate card for each specimen, the whereabouts of the specimen, its registration number and the locality of its collection.

With the Collection there is also a bound typescript of the "Diary of a Collecting Trip to Coen District, Cape York Peninsula on Behalf of H. L. White by William McLennan."

Two large private Collections, the Tom Carter Collection of over 800 specimens, chiefly Western Australian, and the T. P. Austin Collection of over 400 specimens, chiefly from N.S.W., were incorporated by White into his Collection.

The Bird-skin Collection is rich in Passerines (Order Passeriformes: Perching Birds) having good series of such smaller birds as thornbills, honeyeaters, robins, flycatchers, wrens and others, and is understandably, less rich in such groups as the sea-birds (petrels, shearwaters etc.). This must be immediately qualified by recognition of the fact that the Collection contains the first Australian specimen of the Kerguelen Petrel (Pterodroma brevirostris), the first Australian specimen of the Arctic Tern (Sterna paradisea) and for many years contained the only National Museum specimens of the Kermadec Petrel (Pterodroma neglecta) and the Providence Petrel (Pterodroma solandri) and still its only specimen of the diminished Short-tailed or Stellar's Albatross (Diomedea albatrus), from Japanese waters.

Among its Australian treasures are specimens of the following formerly considered possibly extinct and still regarded as rare species:

Night Parrot (Geopsittacus occidentalis Gould) male and female.
Noisy Scrub-bird (Atrichornis clamosus Gould)
Western Whipbird (Psophodes nigrogularis Gould)

A specimen of particular interest in the Collection is its oldest, a Rufous Tree-creeper (Climacteris rufa Gould), still in excellent condition, collected at Perth on October 22, 1842 by John Gilbert, John Gould's collector. This specimen was donated to the White Collection by the Council of the R.A.O.U. in 1923 after its presentation to that body by the American ornithologist Mr. Outram Bangs.

Over 120 different collectors were associated with the specimens in the Collection but a small number of collectors carried out the bulk of the collecting for H. L. White. The following table shows the approximate number of specimens In the Collection from each State and the Collectors chiefly associated with the collecting in each State.

State	*No. of Specimens*	*Major Collectors*
New South Wales	2,720	*T. P. Austin (670)
		*R. Grant (1,000)
		H. A. Blakeney (180)
		S. W. Jackson (160)
		J. Ramsay (110)
Western Australia	2,430	*T. Carter (730)
		G. F. Hill (160)
		F. L. Whitlock (1,250)
		A. G. Campbell (110)
Queensland	1,200	H. G. Barnard (420)
		W. MacLennan (180)
		*T. V. Sherrin (160)
		*R. Grant (120)
Northern Territory	910	H. G. Barnard (270)
		W. MacLennan (370)
		F. L. Whitlock (180)
Victoria	800	R. C. & L. G. Chandler (170)
		*A. G. Campbell (340)
		T. Tregallas (150)
Tasmania	190	*A. G. Campbell (80)
		T. Carter (40)
South Australia	140	*A. G. Campbell (70)
		Capt. S. A. White (40)
Localities outside Australia	150	

*Skins recorded in Register as being part of private collection

The H. L. White Collection contains over 70 specimens categorized as Type or Co-type Specimens. The Type Specimens is the specimen referred to as such in the original description of the species and to which the species name is first attached. A co-type is one of a number of specimens forming part or all of the original material before the author when he did not designate one specimen as the Type Specimen.

Most of the Type and Co-type Specimens in the H. L. White Collection are types of Passerine (Perching Bird) subspecies and the taxonomy and nomenclature of these are at present under review during which time changes of name and of the nomenclatural status of particular names may occur. Whether subspecies catalogued as such in the H. L. White Collection at present retain their taxonomic status or sink into synonymy does not alter the fact that the Collection contains Type of Co-type Specimens for over 70 forms and these are of permanent significance for reference.

The nomenclature of the Collection is frequently carried to subspecific level, i.e. trinomial nomenclature, reflecting the flurry of taxonomic activity in this direction at the period and showing, to some degree, the influence of one of the leading and most active of Australian taxonomists of the time, Gregory M. Mathews. It also reflects H. L. White's early support for the trinomial system, denoting subspecies or geographic races in taxonomy, and a typed statement inside the door of one of the cabinets of the Collection expresses White's supporting attitude in this regard while making it clear that he did not necessarily agree with all of Mathews' subspecific classification, even though he adopted Mathews' "A List of the Birds of Australasia" (1913) as the basis for cataloguing the Collection.

H. L. White was not only a collector. He published a considerable number of ornithological papers and notes including original descriptions of new subspecies or species, e.g. Acanthiza nana flava of which the Type Specimen is preserved in the Collection.

The name "White" has been used as the basis of a specific or subspecific name for a number of Australian birds. In some instances these have referred to S. White (1835-1880) of South Australia or to his son Captain S. A. White. The Northern Shrike-tit (Falcunculus whitei), however, was described and named after H. L. White by A. J. Campbell, and the Grey Honey-eater (Lacustroica whitei) was described and named by A. J. North after H. L. White's son Alfred. (A. J. Campbell had used the name "alfredi" for this form before the description appeared but the name "alfredi", unaccompanied by a description, is regarded as a nude name and does not stand.) The Dorothy Grass-wren (Magnamytis woodwardi = Amytornis dorotheae) was named by Mathews after Dorothy, H. L. White's daughter, and Mathews also proposed the new generic name Harriwhitea for the Albert Lyrebird to commemorate H. L. White. A subspecies of the Rufous Whistler (Lewinornis = Pachycephala rufiventris maudeae) was described and named by Capt. S. A. White after Maude, the wife of H. L. White.

Because the Collection is so substantial and the specimens have been collected over a wide geographic range and over a long period, it is natural to presume that the Collection must contain specimens of virtually every Australian species. This is not so, however, and the items of desiderata are generally not surprising. If we take the current "Checklist of the Birds of Australia Part 1 Non-passerines" by H. T. Condon 1975 and the "Interim List of Australian Songbirds/Passerines" by R. Schodde, 1975 (not yet definitive and thus prohibiting precise estimates) as our standard total list then we can say that a few more than 700 species of native birds occur in Australia plus about 25 introduced species. If we compare the H. L. White Collection with this list we find that about 100 Australian species are missing as also are about 25 introduced species.

Of the approximate 100, however, about 85 are non-passerines, and of these the great majority are sea-birds, (Penguins, Albatrosses, Petrels, Shearwaters etc.) that represent a field of collecting outside the main scope of the Collection, and of which some are very recent additions to the Australian list. Also among the 85 are Terns, Skuas and Waders of the coastal habitats again including species added to the Australian list only in recent years.

Of the remaining 15 (approximately) Passerines, some are very recent additions to the Australian list (e.g. Hall's Babbler) others are extremely rare, e.g. Eyrean Grasswren. The introduced species obviously did not fall within the scope of the Collection in H. L. White's view. Thus of the Australian land birds that were available for collection and that fell within the aims of the Collection, there are not many that are lacking.

H. L. White Egg Collection

The H. L. White Egg Collection contains over 4,200 clutches of eggs of Australian birds housed in a beautifully constructed cabinet of Queensland Maple in eight sections with lettered doors containing 136 glazed and numbered drawers and one additional drawer to hold the sold loose-leaf data book measuring 21 inches by 12 inches by 4 inches. The knobs on the drawers were turned from the Yarran Wattle on the Belltrees estate (R. T. M. Pescott, "Collections of a Century"). It is a magnificently presented Collection and an outstanding one in its coverage of Australian birds' eggs. It is of interest to note that H. L. White's feeling for presentation and appearance led him to depart from one of the traditional practices in housing egg collections. Usually the original data slips that accompany each clutch of eggs are placed in the drawers with the egg clutches. This can, and usually does, detract from the neat appearance of the drawer of eggs and (pers. comm Mrs Judy White) it was because of this that H. L. White withheld the data slips from the drawers of his cabinet and had the data from each copied into the large data book already mentioned. The data slips however were preserved separately and an improved method of filing these for quick reference is at present under consideration.

The eggs themselves, arranged in full clutches are excellently prepared (side-blown) with each egg carrying the set-mark for reference to the appropriate data slip. The data from the data-slips are meticulously hand-written by Mr. Sid. Jackson and Mr. Max Cobb in the loose-leaf Data Book.

Mr. Sid. Jackson, a colourful figure in Australian ornithology of the past, and a renowned egg-collector himself, was employed for many years as the Curator of the H. L. White Skin and Egg Collections and was the one who set up the H. L. White Collections at the National Museum.

The Egg Collection, in the same way as the Skin Collection, is rich in clutches of northern species, and stronger in Passerines than in non-Passerines. Over 380 different collectors are associated with the clutches (sets) in the Collection but here too the bulk of the Collecting was done by a relatively small group of people. Again some private collections were incorporated into the H. L. White Collection, presumably by purchase; examples are the S. W. Jackson Collection and Dr. G. Hurst's Collection.

The following table shows the approximate number of clutches in the Collection from each State and the collectors chiefly associated with the collecting in each State.

State	*No. of Clutches*	*Major Collectors*
Queensland (inc. Torres Str. Islands)	1,300	H. G. Barnard, H. Elgner R. Hislop, S. W. Jackson W. MacLennan, H. Nielson D. LeSouef, G. Sharpe
New South Wales	1,150	A. G. Bassett Hull, H. R. Elvery, F. & D. Jackson
Western Australia	670	C. L. E. Orton, F. L. Whitlock
Northern Territory	490	H. G. Barnard, W. MacLennan H. Niemann, F. L. Whitlock
Victoria	350	D. LeSouef, A. C. Stone R. C. & L. G. Chandler
Tasmania	200	R. N. Atkinson, N. Harrison
South Australia	80	J. N. McGilp, S. White

The first-taken sets of eggs or bird-species are often designated Type Clutches by the collectors by analogy with the Type Specimen of the species or subspecies. This analogy is false in that the Type Specimen is the name-bearer for, and in that sense represents, the taxon (species or subspecies) for which it stands. A clutch of eggs can only be a clutch of eggs of a species or subspecies for which a Type Specimen already exists or will be selected. The clutch of eggs cannot be a Type Specimen and therefore the term "Type Clutch" is an erroneous one. However, it is, or was, commonly used among Egg Collectors as a term to show the significance of the first eggs of a species or subspecies taken and described. In the H. L. White Collection over a hundred clutches are designated "Type Clutches" in this sense, including, for example, the first set taken of the Rufous Scrub-bird (Atrichornis rufescens (Ramsay)).

Again there is the question as to the completeness of the Collection. In this instance it is not a matter of comparing the species represented in the Collection with the species known to occur in Australia but only with those species known to breed within Australia. All but about 25 of such species are represented in the Collection, and, of these, largely Passerines, some such as Hall's Babbler and the Grey Grass-wren have only recently been discovered; others such as the Blue-faced Finch are recent arrivals in Australia. Introduced species do not fall within the scope of the Collection.

Doubt has been raised concerning the authenticity of a few clutches in the Collection and mention of these should not be taken as, in any sense, a detraction from the value of the Collection. All large Collections have their controversial items. Also, in subjecting some of the sets to a critical examination, one does not overlook the vast amount of scientifically correct and valuable data collected and so beautifully preserved. Allowance must also be made for the lack of knowledge possessed by some of the lesser known early collectors and indeed for the enthusiasm of such seasoned collectors as Jackson himself who was, in his earlier days, less experienced and prone to "jump to conclusions" in the field. A leading Australian expert on eggs, who is also an Honorary Associate in Ornithology at the National Museum of Victoria, Mr. N. J. Favaloro, has kindly supplied the following information. Mr. Favaloro's detailed analyses of the sets in question are filed at the Museum and only a listing of these is appropriate here. The queries in general arise from increased contemporary knowledge of the distribution, nesting habits and eggs of species; a knowledge denied to H. L. White and his collectors.

Sets of which the authenticity is queried on the basis of either identification or inconclusive data:

(Current nomenclature is used).

Set No.	
367	Turquoise Parrot (Neophema pulchella (Shaw)) Lavadia, near South Grafton N.S.W.
368	Scarlet-chested Parrot (Neophema splendida (Gould)) Malcolm, near Menzies, W.A.
Set No. 555A & 555B	Tawny Grassbird (Megalurus timoriensis Wallace), (A) Pearce's Creek, near Lismore, N.S.W., (B) Borroloola, McArthur R.N.T.
467X	Mangrove Gerygone (Gerygone levigaster Gould), (includes cantator), Breakfast Creek, Brisbane, Qld.
46A	(Cuckoo Register) Shining Bronze Cuckoo (Chrysococcyx lucidus plagodus (Latham)), Broken Hill, N.S.W.
398A	Spotted Nightjar (Caprimulgus guttatus Vigors and Horsfield) near South Grafton, N.S.W
218	Green Pygmy-Goose (Nettapus pulchellus Gould) Daly River, N.T.

Sets considered to represent error in identity or in recorded place of origin:-

Set No.	
325A	Long-billed Corella (Cacatua tenuirostris (Kuhl)) Nicholson River, N. Qld.
162	Banded Stilt (Cladorhynchus leucocephalus (Vieillot)) Murray River swamps, Vic.
371	Swift Parrot (Lathamus discolor (White)) near South Grafton, N.S.W.
189	Oriental Pratincole (Glareola maldivarum J. R. Forster) Duck Swamp, South Grafton, N.S.W.
164	Eastern Curlew (Numenius madagascariensis (Linnaeus)) Northern Coast of W.A.

276 Black Falcon (Falco subniger Gray) Lavadia, near Glen Ugie Peak, N.S.W.

291 Powerful Owl (Ninox strenua (Gould)) Kingaroy, Qld.

Fifteen sets calling for closer study out of a total of more than 4000 can be regarded only as a remarkably small number. As Mr. Favaloro has remarked (in litt. 24/9/80) "One must look at the work of H. L. White, S. W. Jackson and other collectors employed by White in their proper context. Taking 1918 as the end of the era when books of reference were few and virtually unavailable to field workers outside the capital cities and when the critical examination of museum specimens was almost an impossibility for such folk, one can but marvel at the accuracy of the field work they did . . . For several decades the work of H. L. White resulted in the publication of the most recent and detailed information on birds, their habits and their eggs . . . (and) he permitted his employees (collectors) to publish articles in *The Emu* under their own names . . . The authenticity of a clutch depends so much upon the integrity and the expertise of the original collector, that mistakes both honest and otherwise must occur from time to time. Such mistakes in the early days must have been more frequent when the knowledge of birds and their habits and distribution was in its infancy and field reference almost non-existent. To give a critical opinion upon a specimen or its authenticity is not a reflection upon H. L. White or his collection, but rather an unbiased assessment based upon an understanding of the era, an assessment of the collector himself, and, of course, (upon) reference to data and information available in his day and age . . . As I have said before, we are indeed fortunate and privileged to be the beneficiaries of H. L. White."

An important fact concerning the care of such an Egg Collection and illustrating the need for museum buildings to be as free of vibration as possible, arises from close acquaintance with the Collection over a long period. It has been observed that the vibration from foot-traffic (especially from groups of schoolchildren) on a floor above, and from vehicular traffic in the street outside the Department, causes the eggs over a period of 10-12 years to rotate in their beds of cotton wool to allow the lightest area of shell (i.e. that containing the hole in the side of the egg) to become uppermost. Such movement is undesirable and, for the sake of appearance, the eggs then need to be replaced in their original positions. Eggs of course ought to be handled as little as possible and such handling as that just described ought to be unnecessary.

These two Collections are national assets in ornithology and are not matched in their condition, coverage or data by privately formed collections in any other Australian institution.

For a period during the Second World War both Collections were removed for safety to a country storage site. To ensure safe travel of the eggs fine layers of cotton wool were placed between the eggs and the glass top of each drawer. No breakages occurred.

H. L. White was a true collector who valued both the use of his Collections for the purpose of research and their presentation and preservation for their intrinsic significance and appeal as ornithological collections. They add great distinction to the Collections in the Ornithology Department of the National Museum of Victoria.

A. R. McEvey,
Curator of Birds,
National Museum of Victoria.

ACKNOWLEDGEMENTS

The writer wishes to thank particularly Mr. N. J. Favaloro (Hon. Associate in Ornithology) for the benefit of his expertise in the study of Australian birds' eggs and his historical knowledge concerning the H. L. White era in Australian ornithology. He is also grateful to Mr. Rod Smith (Public Record Office), Mr. R. T. M. Pescott, Mrs. J. Hope Black and Mr. C. P. Vernon (Ornithologist, Queensland Museum) for help in various ways and to the Curator of Birds in all State Museums for their answers to his questions.

Acknowledgement is also made to the Land Conservation Council of Victoria for the use of lists of specimens compiled by Miss Sandra Evans and Mrs. Cathy Jordon in the process of their research in the Ornithology Department.

REFERENCES

For further information The Ornithology of H. L. White by A. J. Campbell, *The Emu* XXVII; 198-200, 1928 provides a bibliography of H. L. White and a list of the field trips made by his collectors and The Diaries of S. W. Jackson and A. H. Chisholm, *The Emu* 58: 101-123, gives an insight into the field activities and personality of Sid. W. Jackson.

"Collections of A Century" by R. T. M. Pescott, National Museum of Victoria, 1954.

Note on Sources

Abbott, J. H. M. *The Newcastle Packets and the Hunter Valley.* Sydney 1943.
Australian Dictionary of Biography, Vol. 1 & Vol. 2.
Australian Men of Mark 1788-1888. Vol. 1 Melb. 1888.
Brady, Edwin J. *Australia Unlimited.* Melb. 1918.
Cameron, Roderick. *Australian History and Horizon.* London, 1971.
Cannon, Michael. *Australia in the Victorian Age*
Vol. 1. *Who's Master, Who's Man?*
Vol. 2. *Life in the Country.*
Vol. 3. *Life in the Cities.*
Connell, R. W. & Irving, T. H. *Class Struggle in Australian History.* Melb. 1980.
Donaldson, Robert. *Life and Reminiscences of Robert Donaldson in his Eighty-Third Year.* Medway, 1932.
Fearn-Wannan, W. *Australian Folklore,* Melb. 1970.
Freeland, J. M. *Architect Extraordinary – The Life and Work of John Horbury Hunt: 1838-1904,* Cassell, Australia, 1970.
Fryer, John (ed.) *Surveying the Hunter.* Newcastle, 1980.
Gray, Nancy. "Background to Belltrees". Gray Collection, Scone.
Gray, Nancy. *The Promised Land. A Summary of Early Settlement in the Shire of Scone.* Scone, 1975.
Gregson, J. *The Australian Agricultural Company 1824-1875.* Angus & Robertson, Sydney, 1949.
Griffiths, G. Nesta. *Some Houses and People of N.S.W.* Sydney, 1949.
Griffiths, G. Nesta. *Some Northern Homes of N.S.W.* Shepherd Press, Sydney, 1954.
Haygarth, N. W. *Recollections of Bush Life in Australia.* London, 1848.
Lang, John Dunmore. *The Fatal Mistake,* Sydney, 1875.
Mathews, G. M. *Mathews Ornithological Collection.* National Library of Australia, 1966.
Mowle, L. M. *Pioneer Families of Australia.* 5th Edition, Sydney, 1978.
Persse, M. de B. "William Charles Wentworth" *Australian Dictionary of Biography.* Vol. 2.
Smith, G. Kinross. *Australian Writers.* National Library of Australia, 1980.
Spencer, A. H. *The Hill of Content.* Angus & Robertson, 1959.
Wentworth, W. C. *The Colony of New South Wales.* London, 1820.
White, Henry, Luke. *Letter Books.* Vol. 1-54, 1886-1927. "Belltrees".

General Reference

CHAPTER ONE

1. "Genealogical Account of Sempills of Belltrees", Glasgow (1832): *Burgh Reports.* (Extract in "Belltrees" Library) p. 49.
   To avoid confusion the modern spelling, "Belltrees" is used throughout, rather than the earlier "Beltrees".
2. "Historical families connected with Kilbarchan". (Extract in "Belltrees" Library). p. 228.
3. Derek Parker. "Eerie Song of the Warlock Craigie" *Paisley Express,* 2.3.1974.
4. Rachel Roxburgh. *Early Colonial Houses of New South Wales* (1974) p. 365.
5. Nancy Gray. "Background to Belltrees" p. 1. (Gray Collection, Scone).
6. Nancy Gray. *The Promised Land* (Scone Historical Monograph No. 3, 1975). p. 35.
7. *Sydney Herald* — November 24, 1834. p. 35.
8. Nancy Gray. "Background to Belltrees". p. 4. (Gray Collection, Scone).

CHAPTER TWO

1. W. C. Wentworth to R. Sempill, November, 1845, ("Belltrees" Library). Transcribed by Mr. Paul Brunton, Manuscript Department, Mitchell Library, Sydney.
2. Ibid.
3. W. C. Wentworth to G. B. White, Deputy Surveyor, Singleton. Vaucluse, March 5, 1846. (Copy, "Belltrees" Library).
4. Quoted in Michael Cannon. *Life in the Country Australia in the Victorian Age* Vol. 2 (Nelson Aust. 1973) p. 194.
5. Michael Persse. "William Charles Wentworth" *Australian Dictionary of Biography*. Vol. 2.
6. Nancy Gray. "Background to Belltrees". p. 7.
7. Edna Hickson. *"George Cox of Mulgoa and Mudgee"*. (Sydney 1980) p.53.

CHAPTER THREE

1. "James White — Death at his residence Edinglassie, Hunter River, aged 41 years". *Sydney Herald,* February 28, 1842.
2. Mss 1008, Mitchell Library, Sydney. See Appendix 1.
3. J. Gregson. *The Australian Agricultural Company 1824-1875.* (Sydney 1907). p. 39.
4. L. M. Mowle. *Pioneer Families of Australia.* (Sydney, 5th ed. 1978). p. 382.

5. Reference. 4.8.1830. Land Deed 30/5888. (Lands Department, Sydney).
6. Nancy Gray. *"The Promised Land"* p. 7.
7. Nancy Gray. "James Bowman (1784-1846)" and B. H. Fletcher, "John Bowman (1763-1825)".
   Australian Dictionary of Biography. Vol. 1. p. 137-139.

CHAPTER FOUR

1. *Daily Mirror*. Saturday, May 7, 1955.
2. Francis White to James Smith Esquire, Police Magistrate, Scone. April 9, 1867. ("Belltrees" Library).

CHAPTER FIVE

1. Robert Donaldson: *Life and Reminiscences of Robert Donaldson in his Eighty-Third Year*. Medway. February 5, 1932. p. 9.
2. Ibid. p.11.
3. Ibid. p. 12.
4. Ibid. p.13.
5. Ibid. p. 14.
6. S. W. Campbell: "Unfenced Cattle Stations in N.S.W. and Queensland in the Early '60's". *Royal Australian Historical Society Journal*. Vol. 6. Part 6. p. 262.
7. H. L. White *Letters*. Vol. 1. p. 49 ("Belltrees" Library). Subsequent references to these *Letter Books* will use the abbreviation — H.L.W. Vol... p...
8. Ibid.
9. Ibid.
10. Sale of "Belltrees". J. F. & H. C. White to H. E. A. & V. White 1889. ("Belltrees" Library).

CHAPTER SIX

1. H.L.W. Vol. 51. p. 223.
2. "Death of Mr. W. E. White — Pastoralist and Sportsman." Unidentified newscutting. 16.1.1914. (Gray Coll., Scone).
3. May Mackay letter to A. H. White, May 1960. ("Belltrees" Library).
4. *Sydney Stock and Station Journal*. 9.5.1919.
5. J. M. Whyte. *"Belltrees" Public School 1876-1976*. p. 2 (Scone, 1976).
6. Alex Cullen: *The Hunter's Head*. Chapter 7. (Scone, 1979).
7. "Ellerston" Store Book 1894. ("Belltrees" Library).
8. H.L.W. Vol. 22. p. 321.
9. Ibid. Vol. 48. p. 416.
10. Ibid. Vol. 26. pp. 460 20.8.1912.
11. Ibid. Vol. 30. p. 40 22.6.1913.
12. Ibid. Vol. 38. p. 84.
13. Ibid. Vol. 39. p. 271 Sept. 1918.
14. Ibid. Vol. 47. p. 846 Jan. 4, 1924.
15. Mark Lee: "History of Bell's Creek Upper Hunter". 1970. (Gray Collection) p.1.

16. Ibid.
17. Ibid. p. 2.
18. Ibid.
19. Ibid. p. 1.
20. Ibid. p. 8.
21. H.L.W. Vol. 34. p. 132 to G. M. Mathews, August 15, 1915.
22. H.L.W. Vol. 42. p. 214 to Purnell, October 30, 1919.
23. H.L.W. Vol. 40. p. 116 to Capt. S. A. White, October 6, 1918.
24. H.L.W. Vol. 35. p. 1011.
25. Ibid. Vol. 35. p. 1013.
26. Ibid. Vol. 35. p. 647 to V. M. White, 1917.

CHAPTER SEVEN

1. H.L.W. Vol. 23. p. 220-222 May 11, 1911 to Frank Smith, Victoria.
2. Ibid. The 50 year courtesy time lag has elapsed after H. L. White's death to permit me to print "private" material.
3. H.L.W. Ibid.
4. H.L.W. Vol. 25. p. 463 to F. L. Whitlock, Western Australia, September 18, 1912.
5. H.L.W. Vol. 46. p. 326 to J. H. Bettington, January 18, 1922.
6. H.L.W. Vol. 42. p. 280 to S. W. Jackson, Queensland, November 22, 1919.
7. *Sydney Mail,* 29.8.1923. "In Partnership with Nature". (Mr. S. W. Jackson R.A.O.U.).
8. Allan McEvey: "Notes on H. L. White Collections". Appendix III.
9. H.L.W. Vol. 35. p. 941 to A. J. Campbell, July 27, 1917.
10. H.L.W. to G. M. Mathews, December 14, 1912.
11. H.L.W. Vol. 25. p. 277 May 26, 1912.
12. Ibid. Vol. 23. p. 222. May 11, 1911.
13. H.L.W. Vol. 34. p. 978 to Sir Baldwin Spencer, National Museum of Victoria, July 10, 1916.
14. *Visitors Book* ("Belltrees" Library).
15. Allan McEvey: "Notes on the H. L. White Collections". Appendix III p.182.
16. H.L.W. Vol. 37 to Mr. Austin, Geelong Grammar School, September 9, 1917.
17. H.L.W. Letter: to J. H. Bettington, March 14, 1920.
18. E. D. E. Van Weenan: *The P.F.A. Quarterly Magazine,* "The Romance of Philately", September, 1917 p. 32.
19. H.L.W. Vol. 46. p. 439. Letter to G. Dickson, Feb. 20, 1922.
20. H.L.W. January, 1918 to Mr. Wright, Mitchell Library, Sydney.
21. *The Sydney Morning Herald* —January 24, 1918. "Historic Stamps — H. L. White Collection."
22. Ibid.
23. Paul Brunton: Letter to Author, December 23, 1980. ("Belltrees" Library).
24. Ibid.
25. H.L.W. Vol. 47. p. 849 to Mr. Wright, Mitchell Library, Sydney, January 1923.

26. *Australian Philatelist* — May 5, 1922. "An Evening with the National (H. L. White) Collection".
27. Paul Brunton: Letter, December 23, 1980. ("Belltrees" Library).
28. H.L.W. Letter: to A. J. Campbell, July 18, 1917.

CHAPTER EIGHT

1. *Scone Advocate.* "Belltrees", August 28, 1900. (Gray Collection, Scone).
2. Family Wills. ("Belltrees" Library).
3. Will of A. G. White. ("Belltrees" Library).
4. H.L.W. Vol. 14. p. 491.
5. Winsome Pender. Letter: October 13, 1980. ("Belltrees" Library).
6. H.L.W. Vol. 18. p. 491.
7. Ibid. p. 256.
8. Timothy McCormick: "Ex Libris Henry Luke White" 1980. ("Belltrees Library").
9. Ibid.
10. A. H. Spencer: *The Hill of Content* (Angus & Robertson, 1959). p. 4.
11. Timothy McCormick: "Ex Libris Henry Luke White". 1980.
12. H.L.W. Vol. 42. p. 90. Letter to J. H. Bettington. 21.9.1919.

CHAPTER NINE

1. H.L.W. Vol. 24. p.203 (August 26, 1911).
2. H.L.W. Vol. 25. p. 405.
3. Michael Cannon: *Life in the Country – Australia in the Victorian Age.* Vol. 2. p. 236.
4. *The Sun Newspaper,* 2.10.1924.
5. H. L. White: Letter lent by Bob Sutherland. (Copy "Belltrees" Library).
6. H.L.W. Vol. 30. p. 832 to Norman Forster, Armidale, March 30, 1925.
7. H.L.W. Vol. 37. p. 189.
8. *The Sydney Morning Herald* — May 31, 1927. (H. L. White's Obituary Notice).
9. "Milroy": *Sydney Mail,* May 26, 1900.
10. H.L.W. Vol. 31. p. 172.
11. H.L.W. Vol. 47. pp. 379, 380 to A. G. White May 27, 1923.
12. H.L.W. Vol. 50. p. 281 to F. L. Whitlock, Western Australia, August 23, 1924.
13. H.L.W. to Mr. Pope, Farmer & Co., Sydney, November 9, 1924.
14. H.L.W. to Mr. V. M. White, London, July 12, 1925.
15. H. L. White *"Belltrees" Station Diary,* 1926.
16. *Scone Advocate,* Friday, June 3, 1927. (Gray Collection, Scone).

CHAPTER TEN

1. H.L.W. Letter: to F. L. Whitlock, W.A. December 24, 1911.
2. H.L.W. Vol. 37. September 9, 1917.
3. *The Corian* (Geelong Grammar School) May, 1915. Vol. 39. p. 50.
4. Ibid. Vol. 45. p. 48. May, 1920.
5. H.L.W. Letter to Miss Judy Coombe, May 1926. ("Belltrees" Library).
6. Maria Parker. Letter. October 24, 1980. ("Belltrees" Library).

Index

Anambah, 40, 54
Arnott, D., 40, 140
Arnott, Primrose, 40, 130-142, 167
Australian Agricultural Company, 27, 29, 32, 41, 95
Australian Museum, Sydney, 85

Bald Blair, 136
Bando, 37, 43, 47
Baroona Station, 37
Bathurst Earl, 27
Belcher, H., 73-75
Bettington, J. H., 88
Bigge, J. T., 27-29
Bowman Dr. J., 30-32
Broomfield, 32-35
Brunton, P., 93

Campbell, A. J., 83
Chandler, W. R., 139
Chandler, Bettine, 130-142, 167
Chester, 38, 39
Cobb, Adelaide, 40
Cobb family, 149
Cobb, Mary H., 40, 54
Cobb, G. F. 56
Cobb, H., 116
Cranbrook, 38, 135
Cronin, T., 150

Dalswinton, 37
Dawson, J., 29-30
Denison, 39
Dixon, R., 17
Donaldson, R., 42-44
Dowling, J. A., 91

Ebsworth, A. C., 88, 91, 96, 98
Ebsworth, Alfred, 96
Ebsworth, Emmeline, 95
Ebsworth, James, 30, 34, 95
Ebsworth, M., 95, 107
Edinglassie, 26, 34, 35, 47
Eipper family, 152
Ellerston, 16, 37, 56, 116
Ellery family, 153

Fairfield, 29
Ferridgerie Station, 37
Forbes, George, 34
Forbes, Sir. F., 34

Garroorigang, 73-75
Geelong Grammar School, 127
Gipps Gov., 25
Glenalvon, 40
Gray, Nancy, 16, 114
Greer family, 153
Grigson, Mary, 50
Greenoaks, 47
Gundy Gundy, 32

Hagen, F., 91

Havilah, 40, 42, 64, 115
Hordern, Norah, 83, 92, 98, 106, 125
Hordern, H. V., 125
Hunt, J., Horbury, 38, 40
Hyndes, M., 134

Jackson, S. W., 76-84, 88, 122
Jarvis family, 133, 150

King's School The, 52, 84, 135, 175,
Kioto, 98, 129-142
Kirkham, 38

Lang, Dr. J. D., 26
Lee, M., 65-67
Leggett, R., 111
Lulworth, 103, 153

Macarthur, J., 30
Macarthur, J., (Jnr.), 27, 29
McCormick, T., 103-105
McEvey, A., 80, 87, App: III
McGregor, J., 67, 148
McInnes, B., 67, 148
McInnes, C., 147-149
McInnes, N., 67, 84, 148
McIver, J., 22-23
McPhee, Harry, 136, 154
McPhee family, 154
Maiden, J. H. 112-114
Martens, C., 45
Martindale, 37, 116
Mathews, G. M. 43, 67, 84-87
Merton, 37
Minell, D., 83, 98, 106
Mitchell, G., 147
Mitchell, J., 22
Mitchell Library, 29, 72, 86, 89, 92, 93
Moran, T., 153
Munro, R., 154
Murrawin tribe, 32, 34
Muswellbrook, 30, 34

National Library of Australia, 87
National Museum, Melbourne, 76, 86,
Noad, W. H., 100
North, A. J., 85

Ogilvie, B., 172

Parry, Sir. E., 30, 34
Payne brothers, 62
Pender, J. W., 98
Pinkerton, J., 56
Playfair, D. H., 139
Playfair, J. W., 140
Playfair, Morna, 130-142, 167
Potter Macqueen, T., 16, 18
Prevost, R., 130

Ravensworth, 30, 32
Richardson, J., 174

Rose, A., 152
Rossington family, 143, 156, 157

Saumarez, 37, 47
Segenhoe, 16, 34, 37
Sempill, H. C., 15-22, 57
Sempill, R., 22-24
Spencer, A. H., 103-104
Stroud, 30, 32
Sutherland, R., 57, 76, 114

Taylor family, 56, 150
Taylor, J., 100, 130, 133
Terreel, 61
Thrift, W., 153
Timor Station, 34, 37

Wallon, 47
Warrior, 16
Waverley, 18, 34, 37, 62
Weightman, T., 152
Wentworth, D'Arcy, 25, 30
Wentworth, W. C., 17, 23-26, 35, 37, 41
White, A. A. L., 140, 162, 172, 175
White, A. G., 47, 51-71
White, A. H., 73, 96, 98, 125-142
White, Camilla, 162, 176
White, David, 165
White, Dennis, 165
White, Edward I, 32, 35
White, Edward II, 30
White, Edward III, 162, 176
White, Francis, 26, 30, 37, 39, 116
White Francis J., 47, 56
White, Frederick, R., 30
White, George, 26, 30, 37, 40
White, Graham, 165
White, Henry Charles, 30, 37, 40, 84, 115
White, Henry Luke, 44, 51-124
White, James, 27
White, James Cobb, 47, 56, 60, 111
White, James, The Hon., 26, 36, 84, 118
White, Judy Lorna, 128-142, 167
White Louisa M., 83, 95, 103-110, 121
White, M. F., 130-142, 158-176
White, Mark J., 162, 176
White, Patrick M., 52
White, Peter, 154, 162, 172, 176
White, Reg, 165
White, Richard, 165
White, Sarah, 30-35
White, Scott, 153, 162, 172, 176
White, Victor, 47, 51-71
White, Wendy, 108, 153, 162
White, William E., 30
White, W. Ernest, 47, 51-71, 120
Wiseman, A., 52, 116, 136, 148-149
Withycombe, R., 51, 103
Woodlands, 47

20/8/84 MCH

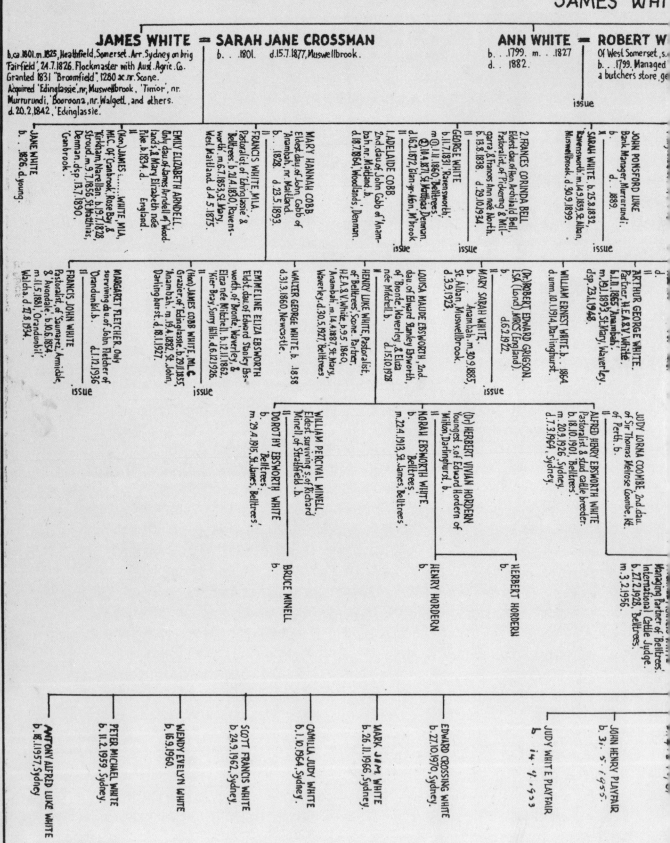

JAMES WHI…

JAMES WHITE = SARAH JANE CROSSMAN

JAMES WHITE: b.ca.1801.m.1825, Heathfield, Somerset. Arr. Sydney on brig 'Fairfield', 24.7.1826. Flockmaster with Aust. Agric. Co. Granted 1831 "Broomfield", 1280 ac. nr. Scone. Acquired 'Edinglassie', nr. Muswellbrook, 'Timor', nr. Murrurundi, 'Booroona', nr. Walgett, and others. d. 20.2.1842, 'Edinglassie'.

SARAH JANE CROSSMAN: b. . .1801. d.15.7.1877, Muswellbrook.

ANN WHITE = ROBERT W…

ANN WHITE: b. . .1799. m. . .1827 d. . 1882.

ROBERT W…: Of West Somerset, s.… b. . .1799. Managed … a butcher's store, ge…

issue

JOHN PONSFORD LUKE
Bank Manager, Murrurundi.
b. d. . 1889.
=
SARAH WHITE. b.25.8.1832, 'Ravensworth'. m.14.9.1859, St. Alban, Muswellbrook. d.30.9.1899.
— issue

2. FRANCES CORINDA BELL
Eldest dau. of Hon. Archibald Bell, Pastoralist, of 'Pickering' & 'Milgarra', & Frances Ann née North. b. 13.8.1838. d.29.10.1934.
=
GEORGE WHITE
b.11.7.1831, 'Ravensworth'. m (1).1.11.1860, 'Belltrees'. (2).10.4.1871, St. Matthias, Denman. d.16.2.1872, 'Glan-yr-Afon', M'brook
=
1. ADELAIDE COBB.
2nd. dau. of John Cobb of 'Anambah', nr. Maitland. b. d.18.7.1864, 'Woodlands', Denman.
— issue (each marriage)

MARY HANNAH COBB
Eldest dau. of John Cobb of 'Anambah', nr. Maitland.
b. . .1828. d.23.5.1893.
=
FRANCIS WHITE, MLA.
Pastoralist of 'Edinglassie' & 'Belltrees'. b.21.4.1830, 'Ravensworth'. m.6.7.1853, St. Mary, West Maitland. d.4.5.1875.

EMILY ELIZABETH ARNDELL.
Only dau. of James Arndell of 'Woodlands', & Mary Elizabeth née Pike. b.1834. d. England.
=
(Hon.) JAMES ……. WHITE, MLA, MLC. Of 'Cranbrook', Rose Bay, & 'Kirkham', Narellan. b.19.7.1828, Stroud. m.9.7.1856, St. Matthias, Denman. dsp.13.7.1890, 'Cranbrook'.

JANE WHITE
b. . .1826. d. young.

Children of Francis White and Mary Hannah Cobb:

d.
=
ARTHUR GEORGE WHITE.
Partner, H.E.A.& V. White.
b.1.11.1865, 'Anambah'.
m.19.1.1893, St. Mary, Waverley.
dsp. 23.1.1948.

WILLIAM ERNEST WHITE. b. . 1864.
d. unm. 10.1.1914, Darlinghurst.

(Dr.) ROBERT EDWARD GRIGSON.
LSA (Lond), MRCS (England).
b. d.6.2.1922.
=
MARY SARAH WHITE.
b. . . 'Anambah'. m.30.9.1885, St. Alban, Muswellbrook.
d.3.9.1923.
— issue

LOUISA MAUDE EBSWORTH, 2nd. dau. of Edward Stanley Ebsworth, of 'Bronte', Waverley, & Eliza née Mitchell. b. d.15.10.1928
=
HENRY LUKE WHITE, Pastoralist, of 'Belltrees', Scone. Partner, H.E.A.& V. White. b.9.5.1860, 'Anambah'. m.14.4.1887, St. Mary, Waverley. d.30.5.1927, 'Belltrees'.

WALTER GEORGE WHITE. b. . 1858
d.31.3.1860, Newcastle.

EMMELINE ELIZA EBSWORTH
Eldst. dau. of Edward Stanley Ebsworth, of 'Bronte', Waverley, & Eliza née Mitchell. b.12.11.1862, 'Kier Bray', Surry Hills. d.6.12.1926.
=
(Hon.) JAMES COBB WHITE, MLC.
Grazier, of 'Edinglassie'. b.29.11.1855, 'Anambah'. m.19.4.1882, St. John, Darlinghurst. d.18.1.1927.
— issue

MARGARET FLETCHER. Only surviving dau. of John Fletcher of 'Orandunbil'. b. d.1.12.1936
=
FRANCIS JOHN WHITE
Pastoralist, of 'Saumarez', Armidale, & 'Avondale'. b.10.6.1854. m.11.5.1881, 'Orandunbil', Walcha. d.27.8.1934.
— issue

Children of Henry Luke White and Louisa Maude Ebsworth:

JUDY LORNA COOMBE, 2nd. dau. of Sir Thomas Melrose Coombe, Kt. of Perth. b.
=
ALFRED HENRY EBSWORTH WHITE
Pastoralist & stud cattle breeder.
b.18.10.1901, 'Belltrees'.
m.20.9.1926, Sydney.
d.7.3.1964, Sydney.

(Dr.) HERBERT VIVIAN HORDERN
Youngest s. of Edward Hordern of 'Milton', Darlinghurst. b.
=
NORAH EBSWORTH WHITE.
b. 'Belltrees'.
m.22.4.1913, St. James, 'Belltrees'.

WILLIAM PERCIVAL MINELL.
Eldest surviving s. of Richard Minell, of Strathfield. b.
=
DOROTHY EBSWORTH WHITE
b. 'Belltrees'.
m.29.4.1915, St. James, 'Belltrees'.

…… Managing Partner of 'Belltrees'.
International Cattle Judge.
b.27.2.1928, 'Belltrees'.
m.3.2.1956.

HERBERT HORDERN
b.

HENRY HORDERN
b.

BRUCE MINELL
b.

JOHN HENRY PLAYFAIR
b. 31. 5. 1955.

JUDY WHITE PLAYFAIR
b. 14. 9. 1953

EDWARD CROSSING WHITE
b.27.10.1970, Sydney.

MARK J… WHITE
b.26.11.1966, Sydney.

CAMILLA JUDY WHITE
b.1.10.1964, Sydney.

SCOTT FRANCIS WHITE
b.24.9.1962, Sydney.

WENDY EVELYN WHITE
b.16.9.1960.

PETER MICHAEL WHITE
b.11.2.1959, Sydney.

ANTONY ALFRED LUKE WHITE
b.18.1.1957, Sydney

…NE BAKER

…SE
…Withycombe.
…, Dunster, Som.,
…y & mill. d.1869.

EDWARD WHITE
Arr. N.S.W., 9.2.1829 on 'Harriett'.
d.unm. 1850.

JANE WHITE = JOSEPH PEARSE
Arr. N.S.W. 9.2.1829 on 'Harriett'.
m. 1838.

(Rev) WILLIAM SKINNER WILSON, BA (Oxon). Rector of Cassilis & Merriwa. 2nd. s. of Very Rev. Dean Wilson of Woodhead, Fyvie, Aberdeenshire, Dean of Aberdeen. d. 31.3.1883, aged 47, Merriwa.
=
JANE WHITE. b. 6.1.1842. m. 14.4.1869, St. Alban, Muswellbrook. dsp.

MARIA SUSANNAH BELL. 3rd. dau. of Hon. Archibald Bell, pastoralist, of 'Pickering' & 'Milgarra', & Frances Ann née North. b. d. 27.7.1923, Sydney.
=
EDWARD WHITE, of 'Martindale', b. 12.10.1839, 'Edinglassie'. m. 25.4.1867, 'Merton', Denman. d. 9.8.1913, Sydney.
issue

2. MARY HELEN McMILLAN dau. of J.C. McMillan of Airntully, Tas. b. d. 7.1921, at sea.
=
HENRY CHARLES WHITE, Pastoralist of 'Belltrees', 'Bando', & 'Havilah'. b. 25.3.1837, 'Ravensworth'. m. (1) 17.1.1861, St. Paul, West Maitland. (2) 10.3.1877, Launceston, Tas. d. 24.2.1905, Painswick, Hobart.
issue
=
1. ISABELLA MARY ANN LOWE, only dau. of Lieut. Alexander Lowe, RN, of 'Bando', Liverpool Plns. b. d. 18.4.1875, 'Woodlands', Denman.

SARAH AMELIA ARNDELL, 5th. dau. of Thomas Arndell of 'Caddai' & Sophia née Loder. b. 18.9.1841. d. 11.9.1933, Armidale.
=
FREDERICK ROBERT WHITE Pastoralist of 'Harben Vale', 'Blandford', 'Booloominbah', Armidale, & 'Timor', Murrurundi. b. 12.9.1835, Muswellbrook. m. 7.6.1860, Pitt Town. d. 6.9.1903, 'Booloominbah'.
issue

AMELIA UNA COX, 4th. dau. of George Cox. b. d. 3.2.1924.
=
issue

≡ Others

IVY BEATRICE VOSS, dau. of Walter Voss, of 'Prairie', Q'land. b. d. 14.1.1956.
=
FREDERICK GEORGE HUNTER WHITE BA (Cantab). Of 'Mittabah', Exeter. b. 18.4.1875, 'Woodlands', Denman. m. 1904, 'Hughenden', Q'land. d. 24.6.1953, Warrawee, Sydney.
issue

2. GREGORY MACALISTER MATHEWS Ornithologist. 2nd. son of R.H. Mathews of Parramatta. b. d.
=
MARIAN CECIL WHITE. b. ca. 1869. m. (1) 18.3.1891, 'Havilah' (2) 6.5.1902, Parramatta. d.
issue
=
1. HENRY JOHN WYNNE, only s. of Richard Wynne of Yarrara, NSW. b. d.

LEILA ETHEL ARGUIMBAU, 5th. dau. of Commander Narcissus George Arguimbau, RN, of 'Cliveden', Annandale. b. d. 31.5.1949, Rose Bay.
=
HENRY HUNTER WHITE. b. 4.10.1867, 'Woodlands', Denman. m. 19.5.1897, St. Aidan, Annandale. d. 1.3.1947, Double Bay.
issue

JOHN WHITE. b&d. . 1872, Muswellbrook.

ADELAIDE JANE WHITE. b&d. . 1870, Muswellbrook.

RUTH WITHYCOMBE. Only dau. of James Withycombe of 'Piercefield', Muswellbrook, & Winifred Jane née Lipscombe. b. ca. 1877. d. . 1958, Knightsbridge, London.
=
VICTOR MARTINDALE WHITE, of 'Lulworth', Roslyn Gdns., Elizabeth Bay. Partner, H.E.A. & V. White. b. 10.8.1867, 'Edinglassie'. m. 10.3.1910, St. Philip, Sydney. d. 1.12.1937, Sydney.

GEOFFREY PECK, Journalist, London. Only s. of Arthur Peck of London. b. d. . 1956, aged 47.
=
SUZANNE VICTORIA MARTINDALE WHITE b. 5.5.1915, Darlinghurst. m. 1939, London. d. 3.11.1969, London.
issue

PATRICK VICTOR MARTINDALE WHITE BA (Cantab). Author & Playwright. RAF (Mid. East & Greece), W.W. II. Nobel Prize (Literature) 1973. b. 28.5.1912.

HUGH DAVID McLEAN ARNOTT, s. of Brig. Kenneth McLean Hardy Arnott, DSO, ED, of 'Glenalvon', Murrurundi. b. 13.4.
=
PRIMROSE WHITE b. 18.1.36 'Belltrees'. m. 20.10.1956, 'Belltrees'.

DAVID HENRY ARNOTT b. 5.11.1965

KENNETH JAMES ARNOTT b. 15.9.1961

VIRGINIA ARNOTT b. 14.5.1959

KIRSTEN ARNOTT b. 8.9.1957

WILLIAM ROSS CHANDLER s. of Jack Chandler of Southport, Queensland. b.
=
VERA BETTINE WHITE b. 1932. Sydney. m. 13.6.1953, 'Belltrees'.

CALVIN CHANDLER b. 10.7.1958.

ROBERT ASHTON b. 1943
=
PENELOPE CHANDLER b. 18.12.55 m 1978

WILLIS ASHTON b. 1981

LINDSAY GODFREY b. 1952.
=
CAROL CHANDLER b. 13.4.54 m.

HUGH GODFREY b. 1980.

DAVID HARDY PLAYFAIR, s. of Brig. the Hon. Thomas Alfred John Playfair, DSO, OBE, MLC, of Sydney.
=
MORNA WHITE b. 1930 Sydney. m. 20.9.1952, 'Belltrees'.

LOUISE PLAYFAIR b. 13.2.1963

N.S.A. Layton, 1981.

29/6/88 Burnett
27/10/88 Wesley Heights